REVIEW FOR THE CLEP* GENERAL NATURAL SCIENCE EXAMINATION

Complete review of skills

By
James R. A. Frendak

This book is correlated to the video tapes produced by COMEX Systems, Inc., Review for The CLEP* General Natural Science Examination by Carolyn Osterberg ©1999 they may be obtained from

comex systems, inc.
5 Cold Hill Rd.
Suite 24
Mendham, NJ 07945

© Copyright   1978, 1980, 1981, 1982, 1987, 1990, 1992, 1993, 1994, 1996, 1997, 1999, 2001

Published by

comex systems, inc.

5 Cold Hill Rd., Suite 24
Mendham, NJ 07945

ISBN 1-56030-135-X

Table of Contents

CLEP* (College Level Examination Program)

CLEP provides a way to determine the level of knowledge you now have in relation to college level material. CLEP does **not** determine your ability to **learn** a subject. People tend to have a **low** evaluation of their ability. There is no way **you** can determine your present level unless **you** take the examination. You can save time and money taking these examinations to earn credit. Others have. Why not YOU?

WHY DID WE WRITE THIS BOOK?

Our firm has conducted many classroom reviews for CLEP General Examinations. Our instructors have assisted thousands of candidates to do their best on them. From this experience we have learned that:

1. In each area there is specific material beneficial for candidates to know.

2. There is a need for a simple-to-follow review book which would help students improve their ability to achieve.

3. It is important for the students to become accustomed to the specific directions found on the examination before they take an examination.

4. It is beneficial for students to develop a systematic approach to taking an objective examination.

5. Many people have been misinformed about CLEP.

These are the reasons we designed this series of review books:

CLEP General English Composition Review Book

CLEP General Natural Science Review Book

CLEP General Social Science Review Book

CLEP General Humanities Review Book

CLEP General Mathematics Review Book

These books will help you, a candidate, perform at your highest potential so that you can receive your best scores.

The flyers "CLEP COLLEGES" (Listing where you can take the CLEP tests and the colleges that accept credit) and "CLEP INFORMATION FOR CANDIDATES" are available free by calling (609) 771-7865 or writing to: CLEP, PO Box 6600, Princeton, NJ 08541-6600.

CLEP INFORMATION

In our reviews, we have found these were the questions most frequently asked by our students.

WHAT IS CLEP GENERAL?

CLEP is a nation-wide program of testing which began in 1965. Today, over 800 colleges recognize CLEP as a way students can earn college credit. Each year over 200,000 persons take CLEP examinations. The testing program is based on the theory that "**what** a person knows is more important than **how** he has learned it." All examinations are designed and scored by the College Entrance Examination Board (CEEB). the purpose of each examination is to determine whether your current knowledge in a subject can qualify you for credit in that area at a particular college.

There are five general examinations. The subject areas are:

1. English Composition
2. Mathematics
3. Social Science
4. Natural Science
5. Humanities

Credits earned by achieving on these examinations replace basic liberal arts credits which are required by many colleges for all types of degrees. Each of these general examinations is very broad in coverage. Questions are from the wide range of subjects included in each of the major disciplines. For example, questions in history (ancient, modern, American, European, Black), sociology, psychology, economics and political science could be included on the General CLEP Social Science Examination. The General CLEP Natural Science Examination might include questions related to biology, astronomy, physics, earth science and chemistry. Because of the broad coverage in each examination, you are not expected to be knowledgeable in all areas. There will be some questions on **all** the tests you will not be able to answer.

HOW LONG ARE THE EXAMINATIONS?

Each CLEP General Examination is 1½ hours in length. Each examination is divided into separate timed portions. For a breakdown of each, check with the specific review book for that examination.

HOW MUCH DO THE EXAMINATIONS COST?

Currently, the fee to take each examination is $38.00. They may be taken one at a time or in any combination. (NOTE: Fees change periodically.)

WHERE CAN THE EXAMINATIONS BE TAKEN?

The CEEB (College Entrance Examination Board) has designated certain schools in every state to serve as test centers for CLEP examinations. A listing of these test centers is included in the back of this text book. Choose the location which is most convenient to you. The **same** examinations are given at **all** test centers. If you are a member of the armed forces, check with the education officer at your base. Special testings are set up for military personnel.

WHEN ARE THE TESTS GIVEN?

Most CLEP examinations are administered during the third week of every month except December and February. The test center chooses the day of the week. A few test centers administer the tests by appointment only. Check with the center where you will take the test for specific information. If you are serving with the United States Military, check with the Education Services Officer at your base to find out about the DANTES testing program. You will be given information about testing as applicable to military personnel.

HOW DO YOU REGISTER FOR AN EXAMINATION?

A standard registration form can be obtained from the test center where you plan to take the examination. Many centers require that you register (send registration form and fee for examinations to be taken) a month prior to your selected date.

WHEN WILL SCORES BE RECEIVED?

You will receive a copy of your scores approximately six weeks after you take an examination. You can also request that a copy be sent to a college for evaluation. The score you receive will be a scaled score. This score can be correlated to a percentile level. These scores **remain** scores until you become matriculated with a college. CEEB keeps a record of your scores on file for 20 years. You can obtain an additional copy or have a copy sent to a college if you contact:

> College Board
> ATTN: Transcript Service
> Princeton, NJ 08541

Include the date you took the test, the name of the center where you took the test, your date of birth and your social security number. Contact CEEB to find out the current fee for this service.

IS IT NECESSARY TO BE ENROLLED IN A COLLEGE BEFORE YOU TAKE AN EXAMINATION?

That depends. Each college has established policy regarding CLEP. You should check with the school you wish to attend. Many schools do not require you be enrolled before you take CLEP examinations.

HOW MANY CREDITS CAN BE EARNED?

Each college determines the number of credits that can be earned by achieving on an examination. Most award six credits if you achieve on a CLEP General Examination.

HOW ARE THE EXAMS SCORED?

See page VII for a detailed explanation of scoring.

HOW ARE THE SCORES EVALUATED?

Before you, a candidate, take an examination, it is administered to college students who are taking a course the examination credits will replace. These students do not take the examination for credit. They take it to establish a standard by which your score can be evaluated. From this testing, percentile levels of achievement can be determined. For example, if you score at the 25th percentile, this would indicate that you achieved as well as the **bottom** 25 percent of those students who took that examination to set a standard.

There is no correlation between the number of questions you answer correctly and the percentile level you achieve. The number would vary from test to test.

CAN THE SAME SCORES EARN A DIFFERENT NUMBER OF CREDITS AT DIFFERENT SCHOOLS?

Yes, because different schools may require different levels of achievement. Your scores may earn you more credit at one institution than at another. For example: if you achieve at the 25th percentile level, you could earn credit at a school which required the 25th percentile level; you could not earn credit at a school which required a higher level of achievement.

CAN CLEP CREDITS BE TRANSFERRED?

Yes, provided the school to which you transfer recognizes CLEP as a way to earn credit. Your scores will be evaluated according to the new school's policy.

CAN AN EXAMINATION BE RETAKEN?

Many schools allow you to retake an examination if you did not achieve the first time. Some do not. Check your particular school's policy before you retake an examination. Also, be **realistic**. If you almost achieved the level at which you could earn credit, do retake the examination. If your score was quite low, take the course it was designed to replace.

IF YOU DECIDE TO RETAKE AN EXAMINATION, six months must elapse before you do so. Scores on tests repeated earlier than six months will be canceled.

HOW CAN I FIND OUT WHAT SCHOOLS ACCEPT CLEP?

In addition to the test centers listed in the back of this text, there are many other schools that recognize CLEP as a way to earn credit. For a free booklet, CLEP Test Centers and Other Participating Institutions, which lists most of them, send your request, name, and address to:

> The College Board
> Box 1822
> Princeton, NJ 08541

If the school you wish to attend is not listed, call the admissions office and ask for information. Not all participating schools are included in the booklet.

HOW CAN YOU USE THIS BOOK TO IMPROVE YOUR ABILITY?

We recommend the following procedure:

1. Complete the review material. Take the short tests included at the end of the lessons.

2. If you do well on the tests, continue. If you do not, review the explanatory information.

3. After you have completed the review material, take the practice examination at the back of the book. When you take this sample test, try to simulate the test situation as nearly as possible. That is:

   a. Find a quiet spot where you will not be disturbed.
   b. Time yourself accurately.
   c. Use the separate answer sheet provided.
   d. When you start the second part of the test, be sure you start to record your answers at the correct number on your answer sheet.

4. Correct the tests. Determine where your weaknesses are. Go back and review those areas in which you had difficulty.

HOW THE EXAMINATIONS ARE SCORED

Let me explain how the examinations are scored. You get 1 point for every correct answer. If you answer a question incorrectly, ¼ of a point is deducted from your score. If you do not answer a question, nothing is added or subtracted from your score. The combination of these totals determines your raw score on an examination. Let me give you an illustration:

If you answer 70 questions correctly you have earned	+70 points
If you answer 8 questions incorrectly you have earned (8 times -¼)	-2 points
ALL unanswered questions are not included in the scoring	0 points
Your raw score is	68 points

This raw score is then computed to your percentile score.

Let us take another illustration:

If you answer 74 questions correctly you have earned	+74 points
If you answer 24 questions incorrectly you have earned (24 times -¼)	- 6 points
ALL unanswered questions are not included in the scoring	0 points
Your raw score is	68 points

Let us take one more illustration:

If you answer 68 questions correctly you have earned	+68 points
If you had no incorrect answers nothing is deducted	0 points
ALL unanswered questions are not included in the scoring	0 points
Your raw score is	68 points

As you can see from the three illustrations, the same raw score developed even though one student answered 70 questions correctly, the second 74, and the third 68. Obviously, the second student hurt his score by wild guessing.

Let us take a look at how this penalty system can work to your advantage. For each wrong answer there is a penalty of ¼ or 25% of a point.

1. If you have no knowledge of a question and you choose 1 out of 5 possible choices, your chance of a successful guess is 20% versus a penalty of 25% if it is incorrect. The odds are against your success.

2. If you know 1 answer is wrong, you are now guessing 1 out of 4, or your chance of success is 25% versus a penalty of 25% if it is incorrect. Notice what has happened. Simply by knowing one answer is wrong, you now have an even guess.

3. If you know 2 answers are wrong, you are now guessing 1 out of 3, or your chance of success is 33 $1/3$ % versus a penalty of 25% if it is incorrect. Now the odds are in your favor. See if you can get a strong feeling for one of the answers. If you feel that subconsciously a particular answer is correct, you should definitely take your guess.

4. If you know 3 answers are wrong, you are now guessing 1 out of 2, or your chance of success is 50% versus a penalty of 25% if it is incorrect. Not only should you guess in this situation, but **you must guess** or you will not be taking advantage of your knowledge of a subject. Remember, you can display this knowledge by knowing answers are correct or incorrect. **You must guess in this situation.**

THE CODING SYSTEM

Over the years COMEX has perfected a systematic approach to taking a multiple choice examination. This is called the coding system. It is designed to:

1. get you through the examination as quickly as possible.

2. have you quickly answer those questions that are easy for you.

3. have you not waste time on those questions that are too difficult for you.

4. take advantage of all your knowledge of a particular subject. Most people think they can get credit only by knowing an answer is correct. You can also prove your knowledge by knowing an answer is incorrect. The coding system will show you how to accomplish this.

5. get all the help possible by using the recall factor. Because you are going to read the total examination, it is possible that something in question 50 will trigger a thought that will help you answer question 3 the second time you read it.

6. make the best use of your time by reading a wrong answer only once.

7. have your test booklet organized for the second reading so you know what questions offer you the best use of your time.

HERE IS HOW THE CODING SYSTEM WORKS*

You can write anything you wish in the question book. You are also aware of the fact that you can think and write at the same time. We are now going to make you a better test-taker, because you will think and write while most people are just thinking.

With a pencil in hand, let us attack some sample questions:

1. George Washington was:

   a.   the father of King George Washington
   b.   the father of Farah Washington
   c.   the father of the Washington Laundry
   d.   the father of Washington State
   e.   the father of our country

As we read the questions we will cross out all **wrong** answers:

   a.   father of King George Washington   NO!
   b.   father of Farah Washington   NO!
   c.   father of the Washington Laundry   NO!
   d.   father of Washington State   NO!
   e.   the father of our country   YES. LEAVE IT ALONE.

The question now looks like this:

1. George Washington was:

   a.   ~~the father of King George Washington~~
   b.   ~~the father of Farah Washington~~
   c.   ~~the father of the Washington Laundry~~
   d.   ~~the father of Washington State~~
   e.   the father of our country

---

*NOTE: MILITARY TESTING -   Because of special regulations for testing under the DANTES testing program, participants are not allowed to mark in their booklets.

Mark your answer sheet and go back and put a big X next to the question, which now looks like this:

X
- a. ~~the father of King George Washington~~
- b. ~~the father of Farah Washington~~
- c. ~~the father of the Washington Laundry~~
- d. ~~the father of Washington State~~
- e. the father of our country

What does this tell us? It tells us the question has been answered and we do not have to reread it. Did it take us any more time? No. And by physically moving your hand you keep yourself alert and working through the examination book. Let us take a look at another question:

2. Abraham Lincoln was responsible for:

- a. freeing the 495 freeway
- b. freeing the slaves
- c. freeing the Lincoln Memorial
- d. freeing the south for industrialization
- e. freeing the Potomac River

Let us go through the answers.

a.	freeing the 495 freeway	No! Cross it out!
b.	freeing the slaves	Maybe. Always read full question.
c.	freeing the Lincoln Memorial	No! Cross it out!
d.	freeing the south for industrialization	Maybe. Leave it alone.
e.	freeing the Potomac River	No! Cross it out!

Our question now looks like this:

2. Abraham Lincoln was responsible for:

- a. ~~freeing the 495 freeway~~
- b. freeing the slaves
- c. ~~freeing the Lincoln Memorial~~
- d. freeing the south for industrialization
- e. ~~freeing the Potomac River~~

Shall we guess? Remember our chart. The odds are in your favor. You are guessing 1 out of 2, so take your calculated guess. Which answer really feels correct? Mark your answer sheet, then put a big X next to the question, which now looks like this:

2. Abraham Lincoln was responsible for:

X
- a. ~~freeing the 495 freeway~~
- b. freeing the slaves
- c. ~~freeing the Lincoln Memorial~~
- d. freeing the south for industrialization
- e. ~~freeing the Potomac River~~

This tells us the question is answered and on we go to the next question.

3. Franklin Roosevelt's greatest accomplishment was:

- a. building the Panama Canal
- b. solving the Great Depression
- c. putting America to work
- d. organizing the CCC Corps
- e. instituting the income tax

Let us go through the answers:

a.	building the Panama Canal	No! That was a different Roosevelt.
b.	solving the Great Depression	Maybe. Go on to the next answer.
c.	putting America to work	Maybe. On to the next answer.
d.	organizing the CCC Corps	Maybe. On to the next answer.
e.	instituting the income tax	Maybe. Leave it alone!

Our question now looks like this:

3. Franklin Roosevelt's greatest accomplishment was:

   a.   ~~building the Panama Canal~~
   b.   solving the Great Depression
   c.   putting America to work
   d.   organizing the CCC Corps
   e.   instituting the income tax

Should you answer this question now? Only if you are a real gambler, for the odds are even. Put a 4 next to it.

The question now looks like this:

3. Franklin Roosevelt's greatest accomplishment was:

4
   a.   ~~building the Panama Canal~~
   b.   solving the Great Depression
   c.   putting America to work
   d.   organizing the CCC Corps
   e.   instituting the income tax

The 4 tells us that there are 4 possible answers left.

Let us now look at another question:

4. Casper P. Phudd III was noted for:

   a.   rowing a boat
   b.   sailing a boat
   c.   building a boat
   d.   designing a boat
   e.   navigating a boat

Even if you have no idea of who Casper P. Phudd III is, read the answers:

a.	rowing a boat	I do not know.
b.	sailing a boat	I do not know.
c.	building a boat	I do not know.
d.	designing a boat	I do not know.
e.	navigating a boat	I do not know.

Since we did not know if any of the answers were wrong, put a 5 next to the question.

The question now looks like this:

4. Casper P. Phudd III was noted for:

5
   a.   rowing a boat
   b.   sailing a boat
   c.   building a boat
   d.   designing a boat
   e.   navigating a boat

Let us try another question:

5.   Clarence Q. Jerkwater III

    a.   sailed the Atlantic Ocean
    b.   drained the Atlantic Ocean
    c.   flew over the Atlantic Ocean
    d.   colored the Atlantic Ocean orange
    e.   swam in the Atlantic Ocean

Even though we know nothing of Clarence Q. Jerkwater III, we read the answers.

    a.   sailed the Atlantic Ocean   Possible.
    b.   drained the Atlantic Ocean   No way! Cross it out!
    c.   flew over the Atlantic Ocean   Maybe.
    d.   colored the Atlantic Ocean orange   No way!
    e.   swam in the Atlantic Ocean   Maybe.

Our test booklet now looks like this:

5.   Clarence Q. Jerkwater III

    a.   sailed the Atlantic Ocean
    b.   ~~drained the Atlantic Ocean~~
    c.   flew over the Atlantic Ocean
    d.   ~~colored the Atlantic Ocean orange~~
    e.   swam in the Atlantic Ocean

Do we take a guess? Not on the first reading of the answers. Let us wait to see if the recall factor will help. But, most important, even though you did not know of Clarence Q. Jerkwater III, what happened when you applied logic to the answers? You have the odds in your favor for an eventual guess. Put a big 3 next to the question and go on.

Your question now looks like this:

5.   Clarence Q. Jerkwater III

3   a.   sailed the Atlantic Ocean
    b.   ~~drained the Atlantic Ocean~~
    c.   flew over the Atlantic Ocean
    d.   ~~colored the Atlantic Ocean orange~~
    e.   swam in the Atlantic Ocean

Your test booklet now looks like this:

1.   George Washington was:

X   a.   ~~the father of King George Washington~~
    b.   ~~the father of Farah Washington~~
    c.   ~~the father of the Washington Laundry~~
    d.   ~~the father of Washington State~~
    e.   the father of our country

2.   Abraham Lincoln was responsible for:

X   a.   ~~freeing the 495 freeway~~
    b.   freeing the slaves
    c.   ~~freeing the Lincoln Memorial~~
    d.   freeing the south for industrialization
    e.   ~~freeing the Potomac River~~

3. Franklin Roosevelt's greatest accomplishment was:

4

    a. ~~building the Panama Canal~~
    b. solving the Great Depression
    c. putting America to work
    d. organizing the CCC Corps
    e. instituting the income tax

4. Casper P. Phudd III was noted for:

5

    a. rowing a boat
    b. sailing a boat
    c. building a boat
    d. designing a boate.
    e. navigating a boat

5. Clarence Q. Jerkwater III

3

    a. sailed the Atlantic Ocean
    b. ~~drained the Atlantic Ocean~~
    c. flew over the Atlantic Ocean
    d. ~~colored the Atlantic Ocean orange~~
    e. swam in the Atlantic Ocean

When you read the test for the second time, start with the 3's. In our example you do not have to consider answers b and d. Do not waste time rereading them. After the 3's, take the 4's and 5's. Keep working. Keep trying to cross out incorrect answers. When you cross out another answer, change the number next to the question. Guess when the odds are definitely in your favor. Do not stop until every question is answered. Do not quit...do not take a break. You can sleep at night knowing you honestly have done your best. I purposely used ludicrous questions to emphasize how the system works. Practice the system as you take your practice quizzes and tests. It is easy to master and can be an invaluable tool in your test-taking arsenal.

You have now completed the portion of the book which was designed to improve your test-taking ability. When you work the practice exercises and take the sample test, use these techniques that you have just learned.

SOME BASICS FOR THE TEST DAY

1. Get to the examination location early. If you are taking the examination at a new location—check out how to get there **before** the day of the examination.

2. Choose a seat carefully.
    a. In a large room, choose a quiet corner. If possible, sit facing a wall.
    b. If you go with a friend, do not sit together.

3. Stay with your usual routine. If you normally skip breakfast, do so on the test day also, etc.

4. If you do not understand the proctor's directions, ask questions.

5. Do not be afraid to ask for a seat change if the person beside you keeps coughing, talking to himself, or doing anything which you find is distracting.

6. Do not quit. Keep going over questions you were not able to answer the first time. You may work anywhere in each section. Beat the examination, do not let it beat you!

7. If you cannot answer a question, code it and go on to the next. Do not spend a lot of time on one question unless you have already finished the rest of that section of the examination. Go through each section and do the easiest questions first, then go back to the difficult ones.

8. **Be sure** you understand the directions for **each** type of test **BEFORE you take the examination**. Not understanding the directions can cause you to lose valuable time when you are taking the actual test.

9. Remember, you can write in the **test booklet. Do it!** This often helps you determine the answers more quickly.

10. Be sure to keep track of which questions you are answering. Make sure you mark the answer at the **same** number on your answer sheet.

11. When you finish—check to make sure you have no extra marks on your answer sheet.

12. Reread the information about the coding system. Use it on the examination. Do not take "wild" guesses. Remember you are penalized a percentage point of a correct answer for each incorrect one. **Do not** be afraid to leave a question unanswered if you cannot eliminate any of the possible choices.

13. Take with you to the examination:
    a. three #2 lead pencils. They should be dull! You are primarily going to be blackening circles.
    b. your social security number.
    c. a watch, if possible. It is helpful to be able to keep track of the time. Sometimes there is no clock in the room—or it may not be working.

Description of the CLEP General Examination in Natural Sciences

The CLEP General Examination in Natural Sciences covers a wide range of topics frequently taught in introductory courses surveying both biological and physical sciences at the freshman or sophomore level. Such courses generally satisfy distribution or general education requirements in science usually neither required of nor taken by science majors. The Natural Sciences Examination is not intended for those specializing in science; it is intended to test the understanding of scientific concepts that an adult with a liberal arts education should have. The examination does not stress the retention of factual details; rather, it emphasizes the knowledge and application of the basic principles and concepts of science, the comprehension of scientific information, and the understanding of issues of science in contemporary society.

The primary objective of the examination is to give candidates the opportunity to demonstrate a level of knowledge and understanding expected of college students meeting a distribution or general education requirement in the natural sciences. Colleges may grant up to six semester hours (or the equivalent) of credit toward fulfillment of such a requirement, for satisfactory scores on the examination. Some may grant specific course credit, on the basis of the total score for a two-semester survey course covering both biological and physical sciences.

The examination contains 120 multiple-choice questions to be answered in two separately timed 45-minute sections, one covering biological science, the other physical science.

The content of the examination is approximately as follows:

TOPIC	APPROXIMATE PER CENT OF EXAM
Biological Science:	
Origin and evolution of life, classification of organisms	10%
Cell organization, cell division, chemical nature of the gene, bioenergetics, biosynthesis	10%
Structure, function, and development of organisms, patterns of heredity	20%
Concepts of population biology with emphasis on ecology	10%
Physical Science:	
Atomic and nuclear structure and properties, elementary particles, nuclear reactions	7%
Chemical elements, compounds and reactions; molecular structure and bonding	10%
Heat, thermodynamics, and states of matter; classical mechanics; relativity	12%
Electricity and magnetism, waves, light and sound	4%
The universe: galaxies, stars, the solar system	7%
The earth: atmosphere, hydrosphere, structure, properties, surface features, geological processes, history	10%

The test includes some questions that are interdisciplinary and cannot be classified in one of the listed categories. Some of the questions on the examination cover topics that overlap with those listed, drawing on areas such as history and philosophy of science, scientific methods, science applications and technology, and the relationship of science to contemporary problems of society, such as environmental pollution and depletion of energy supply. Some questions on the test are laboratory oriented.

Skills tested by the examination include the following:

SKILL	APPROXIMATE PER CENT OF EXAM
Knowledge of fundamental facts, concepts, and principles	40%
Interpretation and comprehension of information presented in the form of graphs, diagrams, tables, equations, or verbal passages	20%
Qualitative and quantitative application of scientific principles, including applications based on material presented in the form of graphs, diagrams, tables, equations, or verbal passages. More emphasis is given to qualitative than quantitative applications.	40%

Biology Review

The Biology section covers all the general information needed to trigger past learning. A more detailed picture of the role of DNA and RNA has been included.

The Cell

CELL STRUCTURE AND COMPOSITION

(Typical Animal Cell)

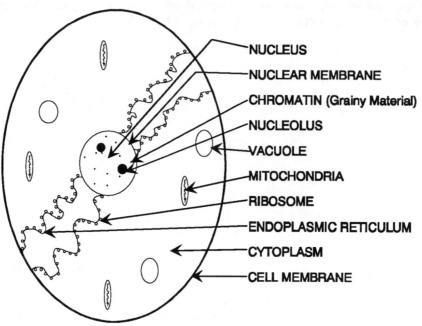

NUCLEUS
NUCLEAR MEMBRANE
CHROMATIN (Grainy Material)
NUCLEOLUS
VACUOLE
MITOCHONDRIA
RIBOSOME
ENDOPLASMIC RETICULUM
CYTOPLASM
CELL MEMBRANE

NUCLEUS

The **nucleus** of the cell is surrounded by a **nuclear membrane**. This membrane is elastic and semi-permeable. This feature allows for the passage of materials both in and out of the nucleus.

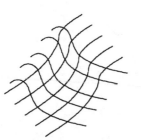

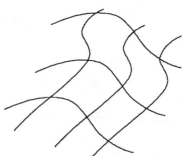

**Contracted Membrane
Small Holes (pores)**

**Expanded Membrane
Large Holes (Pores)**

The passage of materials is selective based on the needs of the nucleus or the cell as a whole.

Chromatin is contained within the nucleus. During reproduction chromatin assembles to form **chromosomes**.

Growth Stage

Reproductive Stage

The chromatin and chromosomes are the genetic makeup of the cell. **Genes** are composed of **DNA (deoxyribonucleic acid)** molecules.

Also in the nucleus are the **nucleoli**. The nucleoli manufacture **RNA (ribonucleic acid)**.

CELL BODY

Other parts comprising the cell are found outside the nucleus in the cell body. **Vacuoles** are used to store water, wastes, or food. The **mitochondria** is the part of the cell where a major portion of the energy needed for cell function is produced. The **ribosome** provides a place for protein synthesis to occur and are often attached to the endoplasmic reticulum. The **endoplasmic reticulum** connects the cell membrane to the nucleus. It transports materials from outside the cell to all cell areas. **Cytoplasm** is the fluid of the cell. It has a gel-like consistency. The composition of cytoplasm is:

(a) Water
(b) Vitamins
(c) Minerals
(d) Carbohydrates   } Nutrients
(e) Fats
(f) Proteins
(g) Nucleic acids

The chemical composition of carbohydrates and fats is carbon, hydrogen, and oxygen. A protein is made of carbon, hydrogen, oxygen, and nitrogen.

Surrounding the cell is the **cell membrane**. This membrane is similar to the nuclear membrane in that it is elastic and semi-permeable.

DIFFERENCES BETWEEN A PLANT AND ANIMAL CELL

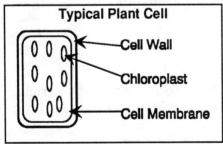

Typical Plant Cell

Cell Wall

Chloroplast

Cell Membrane

Plant cells have a rigid **cell wall** surrounding the cell membrane. It is non-living cellulose and provides "support" for a plant.

Animal cells almost always exist in water environments and can move about freely. Plant cells often do not have that option (movement). Therefore, the cell wall also acts as a protective coating for the cell, especially to protect against dehydration (wilting).

Plant cells also contain plastids (a cytoplasmic structure in plant cells) called **chloroplasts**. These are green in color due to **chlorophyll**. Chlorophyll is an essential chemical in the **photosynthesis** reaction which provides energy for the cell. Photosynthesis converts light energy into chemical energy that the cell can use.

PHOTOSYNTHESIS

1. light + chlorophyll = energy

2. The energy from (1) is enough to split an H_2O molecule, ultimately causing the following reaction to occur: (This is an unbalanced equation.)

$$\text{energy} + H_2O + CO_2 \quad \rightarrow \quad C_6H_{12}O_6 + O_2$$
$$\rightarrow \quad \text{(sugar)} \quad + \text{ release of oxygen}$$

Sugars formed, but which are not needed at that time, may be linked together and stored for later use as **starches**.

The cell performs many functions in order to survive and reproduce. Perhaps the most important activity of the cell is the production of energy. Without energy the cell would not survive.

DNA AND RNA IN PROTEIN SYNTHESIS

DNA (DEOXYRIBONUCLEIC ACID)

DNA strands/chromosomes look like a twisted ladder.

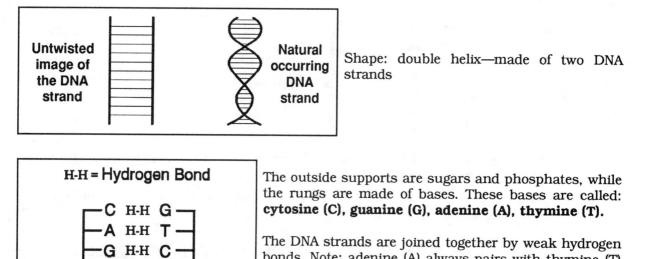

Shape: double helix—made of two DNA strands

The outside supports are sugars and phosphates, while the rungs are made of bases. These bases are called: **cytosine (C), guanine (G), adenine (A), thymine (T).**

The DNA strands are joined together by weak hydrogen bonds. Note: adenine (A) always pairs with thymine (T) and cytosine (C) with guanine (G) in order to form these hydrogen bonds.

The combinations formed by the placement of these bases in the molecule are what determine the functions and/or characteristics of the cell. The most important role this molecule plays is to provide a blueprint for protein synthesis.

RNA (RIBONUCLEIC ACID)

RNA is similar to a DNA molecule. Chemically, the RNA differs from the DNA in that it substitutes **uracil** (U) for thymine (T). Structurally, the RNA single strand can pass through the nuclear membrane out into the cytoplasm. DNA does not have this ability.

PROTEIN SYNTHESIS

Suppose the cell senses a need for energy. A message is assembled by the DNA in the nucleus to make a protein that aids the conversion of stored sugars to energy useful to the cell. The first step of the process begins:

MESSAGE: "Form a special protein at the ribosome."

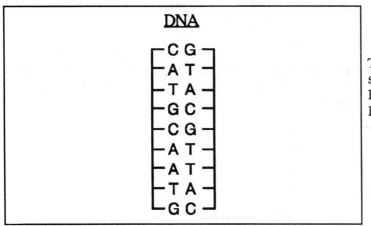

This model is untwisted to keep it simple. The letters represent bases. Bases are connected by weak Hydrogen bonds.

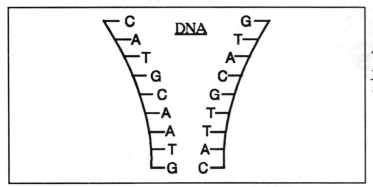

The DNA separates where it had been joined by hydrogen bonds (much like a zipper unzipping).

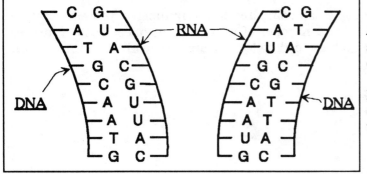

As the separation progresses, the separated ends attract RNA to form chemical base pairs again.

NOTE: the difference between the RNA & DNA is the substitution of uracil for thymine.

The DNA/RNA separate again. The DNA continues fashioning RNAs as shown on the previous page, until it makes a sufficient number.

Chemically, the RNA carries the exact message contained by the original DNA molecule.

ORIGINAL DNA
(double helix) two strands

FINISHED RNA
STRANDS

C G	C G
A T	A U
T A	U A
G C	G C
C G	C G
A T	A U
A T	A U
T A	U A
G C	G C

The finished RNA strands are called **messenger RNA's (M-RNA)**. They disconnect from DNA and pass through the nuclear membrane out into the cytoplasm of the cell. DNA itself is unable to pass through the nuclear membrane.

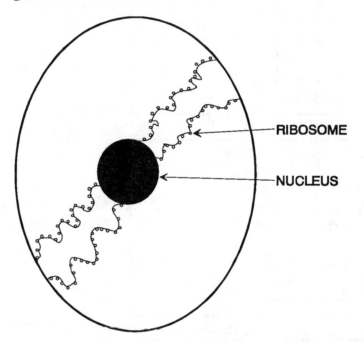

RIBOSOME

NUCLEUS

The M-RNA that arrive at the **ribosomes** is small compared to the number of proteins that are needed. Therefore, each M-RNA attaches to a number of ribosomes at once. Passing nucleic acids (T-RNA units) are attracted and match the coding (complements C with G and A with U).

MRNA C A U G C A A U G

The new strand formed is called a **transfer RNA (T-RNA)**.

Each T-RNA unit carries with it an amino acid. When the units are assembled in the order of the genetic code (full T-RNA strand), the amino acids are linked together to form a protein. When the protein is completed, it is released by the T-RNA.

The M-RNA now releases the T-RNA units and the process of attracting new T-RNA units begins again.

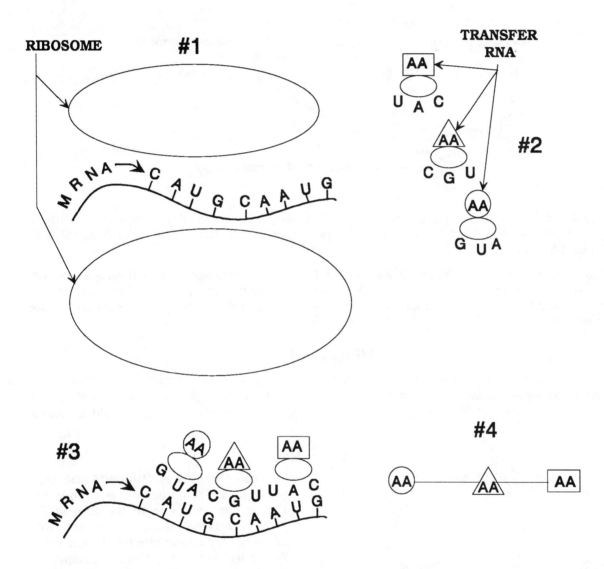

The amino acids link together to form the "special protein" as ordered by the DNA in the nucleus.

ENERGY PRODUCTION IN THE CELL

OXIDATION

When oxygen is in contact with nutrients in the cell, the process of oxidation may occur. Simply, oxidation is the chemical reaction of oxygen combining with parts of the nutrients.

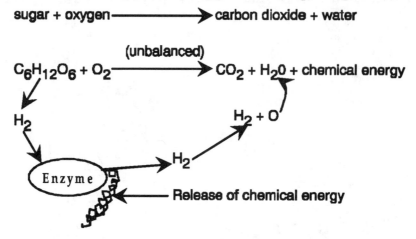

Hydrogen breaks off the sugar molecule and circulates. If it encounters enzymes, chemical energy will be released. This form of energy is not much use to the cell initially because it is such a small amount.

The sugar continues to decompose (2 atoms or 1 molecule of hydrogen) releasing H_2 as shown in the above example. H_{12}—H_{10}—H_8—H_6—H_4—H_2—all hydrogen split off. For now, let us assume that all of the small amounts of chemical energy produced by the reaction of the hydrogen and enzymes is held in the area for some future use.

HYDROLYSIS

Hydrolysis occurs when water and a nutrient decompose and recombine to form new products. Example: fat molecule + water molecule → fatty acid + glycerol. This reaction also releases a small amount of chemical energy. Again, let's assume this energy is held for some future use.

ATP—ADP CYCLE

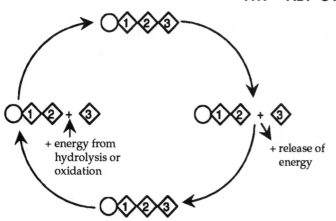

The cell contains **ATP (adenosine tri-phospate)**. This molecule is unique in that it can lose one of its phosphate groups thus releasing a large amount of energy for immediate use by the cell. By releasing the third phosphate group, ATP becomes **ADP (adenosine di-phosphate)**.

The ADP can recombine with the third phosphate again if sufficient energy is available from the hydrolysis and oxidation reactions.

Thus, as long as O_2, H_2O, and nutrients are available, energy production should not present a problem for the cell.

REPRODUCTION

MITOSIS

Mitosis is **identical cell reproduction**. Following are the stages of Mitosis:

INTERPHASE

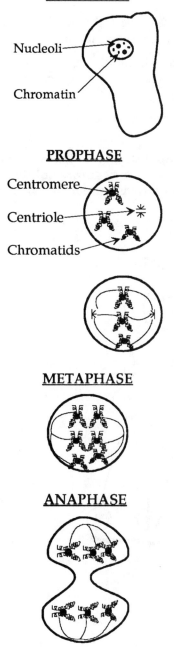

Interphase is not really part of mitosis. In this stage, the cell is increasing its size in preparation for reproduction. It is in this phase that the chromosome are in granular form called **chromatin**. It is also during this phase that the chromosomes divide.

PROPHASE

(a) The centriole is an organelle in the nucleus that divides and gravitates toward the poles when a cell divides.
(b) Fibers called **aster** form and appear to radiate from centrioles.
(c) Chromosomes form as the chromatids thicken and shorten.
(d) Nucleoli is an organelle in the nucleus that disappears when a cell divides.
(e) Chromosomes pair up and are joined by a **centromere** and become visible under a microscope.
(f) Nuclear membrane disappears.
(g) Chromatids migrate toward equator and become attached to the spindle fibers.

METAPHASE

During metaphase, the chromatids are located at the equator of the cell. **Centromeres** join the chromosome pairs.

ANAPHASE

(a) Movement of **single** chromosomes towards the poles (one chromosome of pair to each pole).
(b) Separation into daughter cells occurs:
   1. **Animal Cell**—a cleavage furrow divides the daughter cells.
   2. **Plant Cell**—a cell plate divides the daughter cells.

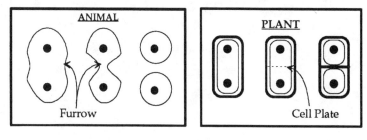

TELOPHASE

Telophase is opposite prophase in that the fibers disappear, the nuclear membrane reforms along with the nucleoli and chromatin.

MEIOSIS

Meiosis is **sex cell formation.**

In meiosis, cell division occurs in two phases. The first phase is called the first meiotic division, the cell duplicates all the genetic information in the same fashion as mitosis.

The second phase involves the reduction of the chromosome pairs (diploid/2n) into single chromosome (haploid/n). It is a further division of the cells without the duplication of chromosome material.

The end result of the second phase is the production of sperms in the male, and an ovum in the female.

If fertilization occurs, a sperm containing a haploid number of chromosomes unites with an ovum containing a haploid number of chromosomes. The fertilized cell, a **zygote**, contains a diploid number of chromosomes. In the diploid state, regular mitotic division can occur and the zygote becomes the kind of living being dictated by the genes.

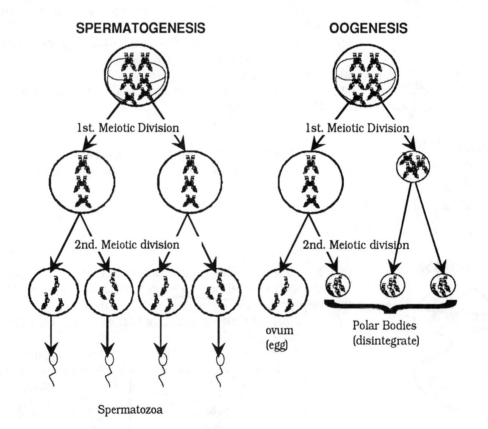

SPERMATOGENESIS   OOGENESIS

1st. Meiotic Division   1st. Meiotic Division

2nd. Meiotic division   2nd. Meiotic division

ovum (egg)

Polar Bodies (disintegrate)

Spermatozoa

Genetics

MENDELIAN LAWS OF INHERITANCE

Gregor Mendel is called the "father of genetics". Discoveries and conclusions gathered from his work with garden peas was published in the early 1900's.

1. LAW OF DOMINANCE

One gene of a gene pair may be **dominant** over the other gene. If so, the other gene is considered to be **recessive**.

EXAMPLE: A pure tall pea plant crossed with a pure short pea plant produced seeds that produced only tall pea plants.

CONCLUSION: The "tall" factor (gene) was dominant over the "short" factor (gene).

TALL / DOMINANT GENE

SHORT / RECESSIVE GENE

Mendel concluded that "factors" controlled the inherited characteristics in offspring. Today, we call these factors **genes**. They occur in pairs and may carry either dominant or recessive traits.

Traits are represented by letters in order to quickly identify characteristics. Capitals are employed to note dominance, and lower case to show recessiveness.

EXAMPLE: TT—gene pair indicating "tall" dominance

      tt—gene pair indicating "short" recessiveness

      Tt—gene pair indicating that the "tall" gene will dominate the recessive "short" gene

Gene pairs are often referred to as being either **homozygous** [genes with similar traits, (a) and (b) above] or **heterozygous** [genes with different traits, (c) above]. The letters (TT, tt, or Tt) are referred to as the **genotype** of the organism. In short, the genetic composition.

The word describing the trait is called the **phenotype** (pure tall, pure short, hybrid or homozygous tall). In short, the physical appearance.

EXAMPLE: Cross between a pure tan mouse and a pure white mouse:

PHENOTYPE	Homozygous Pure Tan	Homozygous Pure White
GENOTYPE	TT	tt
GENOTYPE	Tt Tt	Tt Tt
PHENOTYPE	All hybrid, or heterozygous tan	

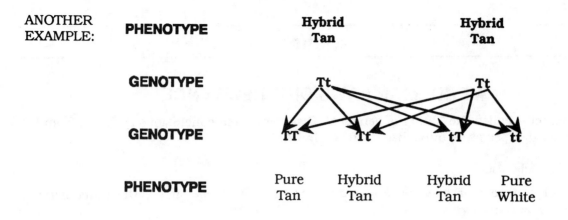

ANOTHER EXAMPLE:	PHENOTYPE	Hybrid Tan			Hybrid Tan
	GENOTYPE	Tt			Tt
	GENOTYPE	TT	Tt	tT	tt
	PHENOTYPE	Pure Tan	Hybrid Tan	Hybrid Tan	Pure White

2. LAW OF SEGREGATION:

Mendel concluded that the genes were separated during the formation of the sex cells (meiosis) and that they (genes) recombine during fertilization.

3. LAW OF INDEPENDENT ASSORTMENT

Mendel concluded that one trait may be inherited independently from another trait.

EXAMPLE: Tall pea plants may produce either wrinkled or smooth seeds (peas)—short plants showed the same diversity.

THE PROTIST KINGDOM

Protists are primitive life forms ranging in size from simple molecules to multicellular colonial organisms. They are classified mainly by shape, locomotion, and method of feeding.

VIRUS

Viruses are the smallest of all living organisms. At best, a virus is a DNA or RNA molecule surrounded by a protein sheath. A virus is "active" only when it is present in a cell. In other circumstances, the virus is inactive. The virus invades the nucleus of the host cell and starts to reproduce itself. Viruses are classified according to the hosts in which they live: bacterial virus, plant virus or animal virus.

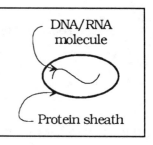

BACTERIA

Classified according to shape:

Spherical bacteria are called **Coccus** (pl. Cocci).

Streptococci are "chain-like" spherical bacteria.

Staphylococci are "bundle-like" spherical bacteria.

Cylindrical (rod-shaped) bacteria are called **Bacillus** (pl. bacilli).

Spiral-shaped bacteria are called **Spirillum** (pl. spirilla).

Most bacteria depend on living or dead organisms for their food. They are parasites (living off a host) or saprophytes (living off dead organic matter). Some bacteria have the ability to manufacture their food photosynthetically or **chemosynthetically** (producing chemical energy by breaking down chemicals—this chemical energy can be used to make sugars and other foods).

Examples of some common bacteria and their environments are:

Live in oxygen (aerobes):	Diphtheria Tuberculoses Cholera
Do not live in oxygen (anaerobes):	Tetanus Botulism

E. coli (Escherichia coli) is a common bacteria that lives in man and survives in both aerobic and anaerobic environments.

Reproduction in bacteria is by fission.

PROTOZOANS

Protozoans are the most **animal-like** of the Protist Kingdom. They are classified according to means of locomotion:

SARCODINA (AMEBA)

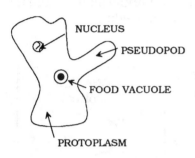

The ameba is unique in that it has the ability to change the consistency of its protoplasm from a gel-like substance to a thick, watery solution. This solution flows from one part of the cell toward the direction the ameba desires to move. The vacated portion of the cell follows along. This action is called **protoplasmic streaming**. The overall movement of the ameba is called **amoeboid movement**.

Amoebas capture their food by enveloping victims with their **pseudopods** forming a **food vacuole**.

Reproduction is by fission.

CILIOPHORA (PARAMECIUM)

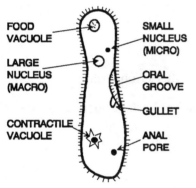

These protozoans have short protoplasmic hairs called **cilia** which are used to move the organism through the water. The oral groove is a unique feature in the **paramecium**. Cilia agitate the surrounding water fanning bits of food into the gullet where food vacuoles are formed.

Reproduction is by fission and conjugation:

A. Fission: Mitotic Division

B. Conjugation:
   (1) Two cells join at the oral grooves.
   (2) The micronuclei undergo numerous cell divisions and the macronuclei disappear.
   (3) Eventually, a large and a small micronucleus exists in each cell. At this time, the small micronuclei are exchanged.
   (4) The cells separate and the newly reconstituted micronucleus undergoes more divisions.
   (5) Two further mitotic divisions occur forming eight new paramecia.

MASTIGOPHORA (EUGLENA)

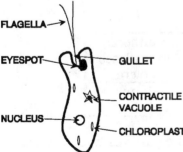

These organisms have one or two long whip-like threads called **flagellum** (pl. flagella). The flagella are rotated and pull the organisms through the water. **Euglena** is a plant/animal. During the periods of sufficient light, the chloroplasts carry on photosynthesis to make food. However, at night or during periods of darkness, food is absorbed through the cell membrane and eventually digested.

Reproduction is by fission.

SPOROZOAN (PLASMODIUM MALARIA)

These protozoans have **no** means of locomotion. They are all parasitic and depend upon a host for food.

Reproduction occurs when the nucleus splits into many small pieces which are then surrounded by cytoplasm. These are called spores. The sporozoan eventually breaks open, releasing the spores which will seek out other cells to invade for food.

THE PLANT KINGDOM

Algae, fungi, slime molds, and lichens are all part of the phylum thallophyte.

ALGAE

Algae are the most **plant-like** of the Protist Kingdom. All algae make their own food by photosynthesis. They are classified according to color:

RED ALGAE (IRISH MOSS)

Red algae are most abundant in warm waters but are also found in colder water. Red algae produce a nutrient called **agar** which is used in the laboratory as a culture medium.

BLUE-GREEN ALGAE (NOSTOC)

Blue-green algae are partial to warm weather and standing water (ponds).

GREEN ALGAE (SPIROGYRA)

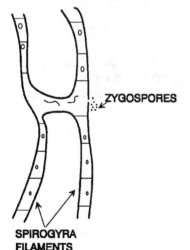

These are the natural plants used in many fish tanks. Spirogyra reproduces by both fission and conjugation. A connecting tube between two spirogyra filaments join. The interior of one cell flows through the tube into the other cell. **Zygospores** are algae cells formed by the combination of two similar gametes. Zygospores are formed and fall from the cell. The zygospores may form new spirogyra filaments if conditions are suitable.

GOLDEN BROWN ALGAE (DIATOMS)

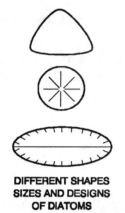

Diatoms are very abundant in the oceans. They are unique for the shell they build around themselves from **SILICA** extracted from seawater. The shells vary in size, shape, and design. They are thin enough to be transparent to light so that photosynthesis can take place. The diatoms store food as oils rather than carbohydrates. It is thought by some scientists that petroleum is oil remains left by deceased diatoms.

**DIFFERENT SHAPES
SIZES AND DESIGNS
OF DIATOMS**

BROWN ALGAE (SEAWEED)

These algae all live in **colonies**. They look much like higher forms of plants having a root, stem, and a flat, leaf-like blade (similar to a grass). Common brown algae are **fucus**, **sargassum** (located in the Sargasso Sea in the North Atlantic Ocean), and **kelp**. At present, some forms of seaweed are farmed for their food value.

FUNGI

Fungi lack chlorophyll and food-making ability. They are either parasitic (live off live plants and animals)or saprophytic (live off dead animals). They are classified according to shape:

ALGAE-LIKE FUNGI (MOLDS, MILDEWS)

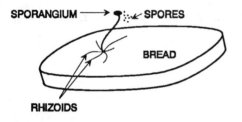

The **hyphae** (rhizoids), similar to roots found in plants but they are not true roots, penetrate the source of food, secrete enzymes which break down the food into usable nutrients small enough to be absorbed by the hyphae. The sporangium matures and releases a large amount of spores which will form new fungi if they land in a moist environment.

SAC-SHAPED FUNGI (PENICILLIN, YEAST)

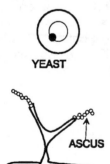

These fungi form an oval sac called an **ascus**. It is in the ascus that spores are produced. Many sac-shaped fungi cause damage to food supplies. Some diseases are: dutch elm disease, apple scab, and many grain diseases.

YEAST

ASCUS

PENICILLIUM

CLUB FUNGI (MUSHROOMS, MORELS)

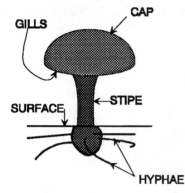

These fungi are characterized by the club-shaped structure which produces spores. The common store-bought mushroom is a good example of this kind of mushroom.

There are many diseases of plants caused by these fungi. Among the many diseases are plant **rusts** and **smuts** whose spores are spread easily by the wind.

IMPERFECT FUNGI (RINGWORM, ATHLETE'S FOOT)

Unlike other fungi, imperfect fungi have only been observed to reproduce asexually.

SLIME MOLDS

Slime molds are similar to fungi in that they produce sporangia and spores. However, they are capable of moving about in a fashion similar to the ameba. Their cells contain many nuclei.

LICHENS

Lichens are composed of layers of fungi and algae living together in a **symbiotic** relationship. A **symbiotic** relationship benefits both organisms. They exist in a wide range of environments because of this relationship. The fungi provides moisture and nutrients for the algae. The algae takes these ingredients and makes food for itself and the fungi.

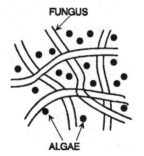

This next portion of the Plant Kingdom review centers around the phylum **tracheophytes**. The plants included in this review are from a sub-division of tracheophytes called **sub-phylum: pteropsida**. This includes the ferns, conifers and flowering seed plants.

Characteristics of these plants include well developed roots, stems, leaves, and sometimes, flowers. Generally speaking, these are the larger plants of the plant kingdom.

Reproduction of these higher order plants shows that the **sporophyte generation** (reproduction by spores) is more conspicuous than the **gametophyte generation**.

FERNS

The ferns have an underground stem called a **rhizome**. Roots grow from the rhizome. The leafy part of the fern is called a **frond**.

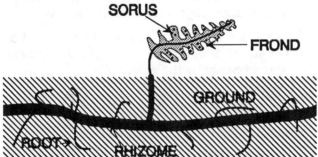

As maturation occurs, reproduction becomes the prime function of the plant. Blister-like **sori** form on the underside of the fronds. These sori contain the sporangium from which spores will be dispersed. The spores may fall into a moist environment and germinate. This is the gametophyte stage of reproduction. At this point, the spore forms a heart-shaped (♥) prothallus where **ova** and sperm develop. The sperm eventually swim over to the ova and fertilization occurs. The zygote is the first stage of the **sporophyte** stage of reproduction. Many mitotic divisions occur ending with the formation of a new fern plant.

CONIFERS

This group of plants includes pines, juniper, spruces, firs, cedars and the sequoias (the biggest trees). These plants are **gymnosperms** (naked seed) and produce woody cones which hold the seed. Most conifers have needles or scales for leaves and stay green year-round. They have woody stems (trunks) and roots. Conifers are often harvested for their lumber value.

FLOWERING SEED PLANTS

This group is the most varied of all the plants and has adapted itself to most environments on the earth. The reason this group has been successful in its adaptation, is its method of reproduction. Seed embryos come equipped with several coverings and a supply of food to keep it growing until it is well established. The flowering seed plants are further classified by the number of "first" leaves they develop.

The **monocots** have a single cotyledon (first leaves). It develops from a seed. Some examples of monocots are grasses, grains, lilies and pineapples. Monocots typically have leaves with veins that run more or less parallel to each other. This group supplies a large portion of the world's food supply (rice, corn, and wheat).

Dicots have two cotyledon (first leaves). Some examples of dicots are carnations, mustard, maple, oak, sunflower and many other plants. Dicots have netted veins in their leaves.

PLANT STRUCTURE

THE ROOT

Roots of a plant serve in the following capacities: to anchor the plant, to supply food and water storage, and to gather water and minerals from the soil.

The root also forms **phloem** and **xylem** as systems for food, water, and mineral transportation through the root. **Phloem** is the system which transports food downward through the plant. **Xylem** is the system which transports water and minerals upward from roots to stems and leaves.

THE STEM

The stem grows upward from the root. In the tree, the stem is called the trunk. However, other smaller plant's stems are similar to the tree trunk.

A **woody** stem contains:
1. **bark** for protection and to prevent water loss through evaporation;
2. **cambium** which forms **xylem** and **phloem**;
3. **wood** for the conduction of food, water and minerals;
4. **pith** for the storage of food.

THE LEAF

Leaves manufacture food for the plant. Generally, leaves contain: a covering called the **cuticle**; many **stomata** (holes) to regulate water through photosynthesis and carbon dioxide levels; **palisade cells** which manufacture the food through photosynthesis; and **veins** made of xylem and phloem.

FLOWERING PLANT REPRODUCTION

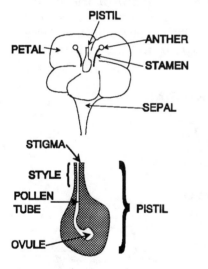

PISTIL - sticky top called a **stigma**; tube called a **style**; base called an **ovary**. This is the female part of the flower.

STAMEN - stalk that supports the **anther** which contains the **pollen**. This is the male part of the flower.

Pollen matures into sperm which make their way to the **ovule**. There, fertilization occurs and a zygote is formed. After fertilization occurs, the plant puts all its energy into seed or fruit production. Example: berries, apples, nuts, grains, etc.

THE ANIMAL KINGDOM

PORIFERA (SPONGES)

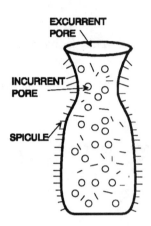

EXCURRENT PORE

INCURRENT PORE

SPICULE

Sponges are filled with holes. Sponge cells draw water through the holes (called **incurrent pores**) and remove nutrients as well as oxygen before returning the water to its surroundings through larger holes (called **excurrent pores**).

Cells of a sponge are arranged in two layers. On the outside, there are **epidermal** cells for protection. Inside, there are cells known as **collar cells**.

Each collar cell has a flagellum which fans water into its collar. Here, food and oxygen are removed and passed along to cells called **amebocytes** which distribute the nutrients to other cells.

COLLAR CELL

Sponges have **spicules** which are calcareous that make up the skeleton of the sponge.

SPICULE

Sponges may reproduce by **budding** (reproduction by breaking off a piece of the original to form two individuals) and **regeneration** (replacing tissue that is lost). They may also reproduce sexually by releasing sperm in the water. The sperm swim around and enter other sponges and fertilize ova. The zygote eventually develops into a "free swimmer" that will eventually settle to the ocean floor and become a sponge.

COELENTERATES (JELLYFISH, CORALS, HYDRA)

PLANULA

POLYP

ROCK

Coelenterates exist in various body shapes during their life span. Some begin life as free-swimming **planula**. Planula are larva of coelenterates and may develop into a polyp shape (hydra) or into a **medusa** (mature coelenterate that lacks means of self propulsion)—both adult forms of coelenterates are able to reproduce. Other planula alternate generations—develop into polyps which produce planula that develop into medusas which produce planula that develop into polyps, etc.

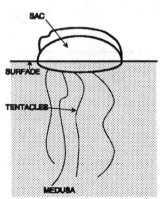

SAC

SURFACE

TENTACLES

MEDUSA

Coelenterates contain two layers of cells separated by a jelly-like substance called **mesoglea**. The stinging cells located in the **tentacles** are called **nematocysts**. Food is obtained when a victim is paralyzed by several stings from the nematocysts. Slowly, food is drawn into a gastrovascular cavity (in polyps) where it is digested. Reproduction may occur through budding, regeneration or sexual activity.

ROTIFERA

Rotifera are cylindrical-shaped, multi-cellular organisms that live in fresh water. They possess **cilia** around the mouth(s) which draw nutrients into their well developed digestive systems.

PLATYHELMINTHES (FLATWORMS—PLANARIA)

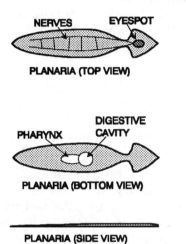

NERVES EYESPOT

PLANARIA (TOP VIEW)

PHARYNX DIGESTIVE CAVITY

PLANARIA (BOTTOM VIEW)

PLANARIA (SIDE VIEW)

Life beyond Rotifera has three layers of cells: **ectoderm**, **mesoderm** and **endoderm**.

The planarian (flatworm) is a free-swimmer which sucks its food through the pharynx tube.

It may reproduce by asexual (fission) or sexual means. The animal contains both male and female sex organs (hermaphroditic) so cross fertilization is easily accomplished.

The planarian has marvelous powers of regeneration because it can regenerate up to half its body.

NEMATODES (ROUND WORMS—TRICHINA, HOOK WORM)

One of the major differences between round and flatworms is their body shape. Round worms are tubular and contain a digestive cavity that runs the length of the body (mouth to anus). The flatworms have a short digestive system with one opening which serves as an entrance for food and an exit for wastes. Many of the parasitic worms that infect animals are round worms.

ANNELIDS (SEGMENTED WORMS—EARTHWORM)

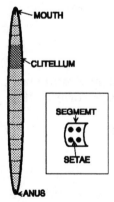

MOUTH

CLITELLUM

SEGMEMT

SETAE

ANUS

The earthworm has well developed digestive, excretory, circulatory, nervous, muscular, and reproductive systems.

The digestive system contains a **gizzard** which grinds up the soil the earthworm swallows. Digestive enzymes attack the finely ground up soil extracting nutrients to be distributed the length of the body by the circulating blood.

Earthworms have "grippers" called **setae** on their underside. Reproduction is sexual. The earthworm is hermaphroditic.

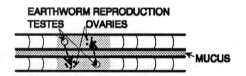

EARTHWORM REPRODUCTION
TESTES OVARIES

MUCUS

LARGE ARROWS INDICATE THE DIRECTION OF THE SPERM EXCHANGE

MOLLUSKS (SHELLFISH)

Mollusks have soft bodies and possess an outer layer of cells called a **mantle**.

PELECYPODS [BI-VALVES (TWO SHELLS)—CLAMS, OYSTERS]

Bi-valves contain **siphon tubes**—incurrent and excurrent. Water is constantly circulated in and out of the shell cavity to obtain oxygen at the gills and food at the mouth. Wastes are removed by water circulating over the gills to remove carbon dioxide and food wastes at the anus.

GASTROPODS ("STOMACH FOOT"—SNAILS)

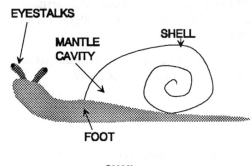

SNAIL

These animals have only **one shell**. (Slugs have none at all!)

The gastropod "breathes" through the exchange of gases in the **mantle cavity**. It is able to move by secreting a slime and contracting the foot muscle. Eating is accomplished by scraping its **radula** (made of chitin) against leaves and digesting nutrients in the digestive system. The radula is in the mouth of a mollusk and is used to grind up food.

CEPHALOPODS ("HEAD FOOT"—OCTOPUS, SQUID)

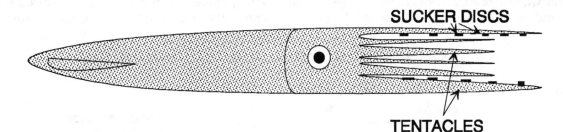

These are free-swimmers that use "jet-propulsion" to move around their marine environments. Tentacles have sucker discs which aid the cephalopod's "attaching" itself to rocks or crawling about on the ocean floor.

ARTHROPODS (JOINTED FOOT)

All arthropods have the following common characteristics:

1. A hard outer body shell called an **exoskeleton**. This exoskeleton is made of a substance called **chitin**.

2. These are the first animals to have **jointed appendages**.

3. There are four classifications of arthropods:
    a. Myriapoda
    b. Insects
    c. Crustaceans
    d. Arachnids

MYRIAPODA (MANY FEET—CENTIPEDES, MILLIPEDES)

 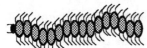

**CENTIPEDE
TWO LEGS PER
SEGMENT**

**MILLIPEDE
FOUR LEGS PER
SEGMENT**

Centipedes have jointed appendages for almost all of their segments; millipedes have jointed appendages for all segments. Centipedes are carnivorous and contain poison claws which enable them to capture food. Millipedes are mainly herbivorous.

INSECTS (MOSQUITOS, FLIES)

Insects have three major body parts: head, thorax, abdomen. They also have: six legs; breathing tubes called **spiracles** located in the abdomen; a pair of antenna; and two pairs of wings.

The insect life-cycle, coupled with wings and special feeding parts, has allowed insects to inhabit all but the coldest portions of the earth's surface.

Insects undergo a **metamorphosis** (change in body shape) from egg through to adult form.
1. egg
2. larva (worm-like—caterpillar, etc.)
3. pupa (change from worm-like form to adult form)
4. adult

Insect eggs that hatch into small adult forms, called **nymphs**, are **bugs**. A good example of a bug is a grasshopper.

CRUSTACEANS (LOBSTER, CRAB, SHRIMP)

Crustaceans have two body parts: cephalothorax and abdomen. They have gills, many appendages, and are the largest of the Arthropods.

ARACHNIDS (SPIDERS, SCORPION, HORSE-SHOE CRAB, MITES AND TICKS)

Arachnids have two body parts: cephalothorax and abdomen. Spiders have **book lungs**, no antennae, and eight legs (common to all arachnids).

ECHINODERMS (STARFISH)

STARFISH

**UNDERSIDE
STARFISH**

SUCKER DISK **TUBE FOOT**

WATER VASCULAR SYSTEM

Starfish have hard, spiny bodies. The underside of the **rays** of the starfish have two rows of **tube feet**. These feet are manipulated by a **water vascular system**. Water pumped into this system causes the **suction discs** to puff out releasing its grip on the surface. By rhythmically moving the water through the system, alternating the attachment/release of the discs, the starfish is able to move through the water.

The tube feet are also used to capture oysters or clams for food. By attaching the tube feet and pulling slowly, the shellfish's shells separate enough to allow the starfish to slip its stomach inside the shells and digest the contents.

Reproduction is sexual with male and female starfish releasing sperm and ova into the water. Fertilization occurs and produces ciliated larva which eventually settle to the bottom and assume the radially symmetrical shape and body parts of the starfish.

CHORDATES

Chordates contain three prominent features at some time in their lives:

1. **notochord**—hard, internal, supporting rod of connective tissue.
2. **paired gill slits**—become gills in fish and amphibians; disappear in other chordates (including man).
3. **a dorsal nerve cord**—spinal cord.

The following list of **chordates** are all vertebrates (animals with backbones).

PISCES (FISH)

They have gills for breathing, fins for locomotion, a two-chambered heart, and external fertilization.

AMPHIBIAN (FROG)

They undergo metamorphosis from **tadpole** to **frog**. The tadpole has a long swimming tail, yolk sac, gills, and a two-chambered heart, but no legs. The frog has **no** tail, four legs (two large powerful back legs and two smaller front legs), lungs, three-chambered heart. Fertilization takes place externally.

REPTILES (TURTLE, ALLIGATOR, SNAKE)

Reptiles have a four-chambered heart, four legs (snake has the bones but **no** legs), thick, scaly skin. These animals have internal fertilization.

AVES (BIRDS)

Birds have feathers, four-chambered hearts (first of the warm-blooded animals), wings, and fertilization occurs internally.

One of the more interesting adaptations to the environment is exhibited by birds. They possess specialized beaks, legs and feet that are adapted to their method of feeding. Examples: seed eaters (chickadee), insect eaters (swallow), strainers (duck), fish eaters (diving birds), meat eaters (eagles, hawks), birds that inhabit swamps (long legs and beaks, very wide-spread claws on their feet—i.e., egrets).

MAMMALS (BAT, WHALE, PORPOISE, PLATYPUS, KANGAROO, MAN, ETC.)

Mammals possess a body covering of hair, four-chambered hearts, a diaphragm to separate the chest cavity from the digestive cavity, a highly developed brain, and **mammary glands** which provide nourishment (milk) for the newborn.

Systems: Higher Levels Of Organization—Human

REPRODUCTIVE SYSTEM

MALE

Sex cells are produced in the **testes**. They grow tails and are called **sperm** or **spermatozoa**. The tail's function is to provide locomotion in the fluid called **semen**.

Testes are held in a sac called the **scrotum** which is located below and outside the abdomen. The location is critical because sperm production and storage is best at lower than body temperature which is 98.6° F.

The duct system from the testes through the penis involves the **epididymis**, **vas deferens**, **ejaculatory duct**, and **urethra**. The sperm travel through this passageway of ducts to exit the male body.

The **prostate** and **seminal vesicles** provide **semen** and chemicals to activate the sperm.

FEMALE

Sex cells are produced in the **ovaries**. Female sex cells have no means of locomotion. They are called **ova** (pl.). The ovaries are located in the lower abdominal cavity and produce the hormones **estrogen** and **progesterone**. An egg (ovum) is passed from the ovary to the **fallopian tube** (oviduct) where it is moved along by the ciliated lining of the tube. The **uterus** receives the ovum. If the egg is not fertilized, the female will experience **menstruation** when the inner layers of the uterus are discharged. If fertilization has occurred in the fallopian tubes, the **zygote** attaches to the walls of the uterus and grows into a **fetus**. Hormones will be released to keep the woman from going through menstration.

The **vagina** is the cavity that receives semen from the male. It also discharges menstrual flow and is the passageway for birth. External features include the **vulva** (labia majora, labia minora) which encloses the vagina, and the **clitoris** which is a small erectile, sensitive tissue.

CIRCULATORY SYSTEM

The function of the circulatory system is to provide the flow of materials through the body. Circulation provides for the exchange of gases (O_2-CO_2), removal of wastes, regulation of body temperature, nutrition, H_2O regulation as well as proper pH maintenance, and immune protection (white blood cells and antibodies).

The **plasma** contains water, carbonates, chlorides, phosphates, urea, hormones, vitamins, digested food, albumin, globulin, fibrinogen, and prothrombin.

There are three different types of blood cells.

1. **Red blood corpuscles (erythrocytes)**—the main function of the cell is to transport hemoglobin within the cell. Hemoglobin is a chemical that readily combines and dissassociates from oxygen depending on surrounding concentrations of oxygen. Mature cells have no nucleus.

2. **White blood corpuscles (leukocytes)**—this cell has no hemoglobin. It has an **ameboid** shape and method of locomotion. The main function is to provide immune protection to the body.

3. **Platelets (thrombocytes)**—the main function is **clotting**.

All of the blood cells are produced in the **bone marrow** with the exception of leukocytes, which may also form in the **spleen**.

Vessels carrying blood include:

1. from heart to body: **aorta, arteries, arterioles** (the smallest arteries)

2. **capillaries**—small blood vessels connecting arterioles to vennoles

3. from body to heart: **veinules** (the smallest veins), **veins**

Arteries have thick walls and pulsate, pushing blood through the body. The capillaries connect the arterial system to the **venous** system. Veins have thin walls and valves which prevent the blood from flowing backward.

The **heart** is a muscular pump which causes the blood to circulate through the body. It is **cone-shaped** and has walls which have three layers of muscle tissue: **endocardium, myocardium**, and **pericardium**.

Blood flows back to the heart from all parts of the body. The **venae cavae** empty into the **right atrium** of the heart. Blood flows to the **right ventricle** and then out to the lungs through the **pulmonary arteries** (the only **non-oxygenated arterial blood in the body**). After the exchange of gases in the lungs, blood returns through the **pulmonary veins (oxygenated blood)** to the **left atrium**, then to the **left ventricle** and out to the body through the **aorta**.

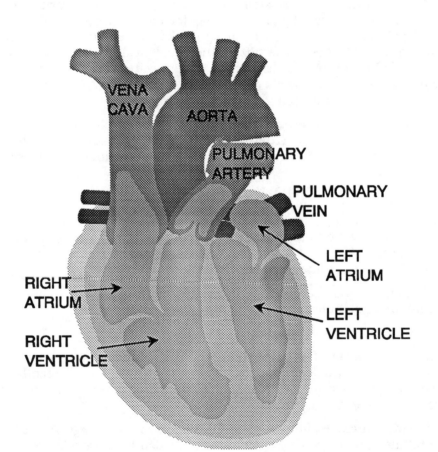

ENDOCRINE SYSTEM

This system is made up of glands in the body that secrete **hormones** to regulate body functions. The hormones are released into the circulatory system and carried throughout the body.

1. **Pituitary gland**—located in the brain, it regulates or activates the following:
   (a) growth
   (b) cortex (the outer portion of the brain) activity
   (c) thyroid activity
   (d) H_2O in the blood
   (e) ovary or sperm development
   (f) corpus luteum (a ductless gland in the ovary) and testosterone

2. **Pineal gland**—located in the brain, it regulates ovaries and is the "biological clock" of the body.

3. **Thyroid gland**—located in the neck, it regulates metabolic rate and calcium concentration in the blood.

4. **Parathyroid gland**—located on the backside of the thyroid, it regulates calcium in the blood.

5. **Adrenal gland**—located on the top of the kidneys, it regulates potassium and sodium in the blood, heartbeat, blood pressure, and blood sugar level.

6. **Pancreas**—located below stomach, it regulates passage of sugar into the cells.

7. **Ovaries**—located in pelvis of the female, it regulates the development of sex organs and characteristics.

8. **Testes**—located below pelvis in the male.

9. **Thymus**—located in chest, its function is unknown.

NERVOUS SYSTEM

This system consists of the **brain**, **spinal cord** and **nerves**. The function of this system is to regulate and coordinate body activities.

There are two main divisions in this system:

1. **central nervous system**—which causes voluntary movement.

2. **autonomic nervous system**—which regulates heartbeat, glands, and smooth muscles.

EXCRETORY SYSTEM

This system eliminates toxic or excessive by-products of metabolism.

In man, excess CO_2 that builds up from the metabolism of food is removed from the body by the lungs. The **kidneys** are the primary excretory organs for other products of metabolism. The kidneys remove the end-products of digestion, some excess H_2O, vitamins, hormones and enzymes. They also convert **urea** to **urine** in order to discharge waste from the body.

MUSCULAR SYSTEM

This system contains **voluntary** and **involuntary** muscles. Voluntary muscles are **striated** and are used for fast contraction. Involuntary muscles include **smooth** and **cardiac** muscle. Smooth muscle contraction is slow. Cardiac muscle contracts in a regular fashion and does not tire easily.

RESPIRATORY SYSTEM

This is the process by which cells receive O_2 and give off CO_2. The steps involved in respiration are:

1. **breathing**—movement of air in and out of the lungs.

2. **external respiration**—exchange of gases (O_2 - CO_2) in the lungs.

3. **transpiration**—movement of O_2 - CO_2 by blood to and from cells.

4. **internal respiration**—exchange of gases between the cells and the blood.

Oxygen is used with nutrients in the cell to produce usable energy.

INTEGUMENTARY SYSTEM

The **skin** provides an outer protective covering.

DIGESTIVE SYSTEM

This is the process which changes large organic molecules into smaller organic molecules that can pass through cell membranes. **Enzymes** are responsible for this process.

1. **Mouth**—contains **teeth** and **tongue**. Secretes **mucus** and **saliva** and begins the breakdown of food by enzymes.

2. **Esophagus**—moves food to stomach area.

3. **Stomach**—churns food and mixes in **gastric juices** and **hydrochloric acid** to further break down food.

4. **Small intestine**—more secretions are added here. They include **pancreatic juice**, **bile**, and **intestinal juices**. Food is broken into usable molecules and taken away by the blood.

5. **Large intestine** (colon)—undigested food and unusable solids (feces) make their way out of the body through the anus.

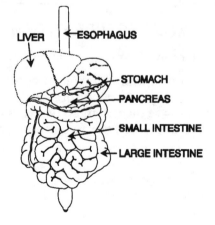

Chemistry Review

The chemistry covered in this section will provide you with a working knowledge of this science. It is basic and can be learned by anyone. It is not necessary to have had a formal course in chemistry to be able to understand this material.

The section dealing with radioactivity covers a number of sciences in addition to chemistry.

Structure and Composition of the Atom

Atoms are the smallest part an element can be broken into, while retaining all of the properties of that element. **Atoms** are made of three large particles. These particles occupy specific locations in the atom.

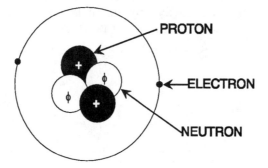

ATOMIC WEIGHT

Protons and **neutrons** are located in the **nucleus** of the atom. Each of these particles weighs approximately one **amu** (atomic mass unit, a relative weight). Together they constitute the **atomic weight** of the atom.

Often atomic weight will accompany the chemical symbol in texts or tests. The atomic weight is placed to the upper right of the symbol. Example: U^{238}, H^1, O^{16}. 238, 1 and 16 indicate the atomic weights of these atoms.

ISOTOPES

An atom is defined by the number of protons. Although the atoms of the same element contain the same number of protons, the number of neutrons may vary. Therefore, Uranium may be expressed as U^{238}, U^{235}, or U^{234}, depending upon the specific atomic weight. These U atoms can be referred to as **isotopes**.

Many atoms have isotopic forms.

EXAMPLE: The isotopes below are hydrogen because they have one proton and electron. But, they all are isotopes of hydrogen because they are different atomic weights of the same element.

ISOTOPES OF HYDROGEN

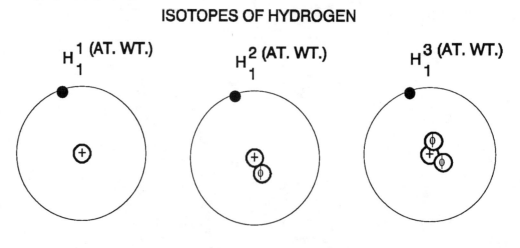

EXAMPLE: The isotopes below are uranium because they have 92p⁺ and 92e⁻. But, they all are isotopes of uranium because they are different atomic weights of the same element.

ISOTOPES OF URANIUM

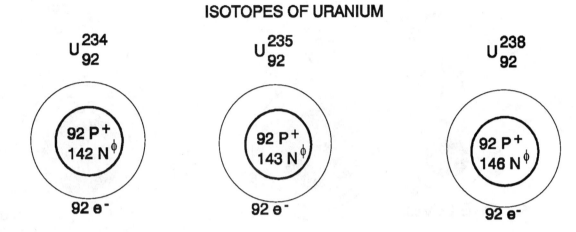

U_{92}^{234} U_{92}^{235} U_{92}^{238}

92 P⁺
142 N^φ   92 P⁺
143 N^φ   92 P⁺
146 N^φ

92 e⁻   92 e⁻   92 e⁻

ATOMIC NUMBER—PROTONS

The number of protons in the nucleus determines the **atomic number** of the atom. Each element (group of similar atoms) has its own atomic number. When this number accompanies the chemical symbol, it is placed to the lower right of the symbol.

EXAMPLE:

at. wt.
↙
H_1^1 U_{92}^{238} Li_3^7
↖
at. no.

ELECTRICAL CHARGES OF THE ATOM

The atomic number, or the number of protons in the nucleus, determines the number of electrons present in an **atom**. Atoms are electrically **neutral**. For every proton there is an electron. The positive electrical charge of the proton is cancelled by the negative electrical charge of the electron. In an atom, the number of positive (+) charges = the number of negative (-) charges, leaving the atom in a neutral electrical state.

ELECTRONS

Electrons are located outside the nucleus at sites called rings/orbits/shells/levels (take your choice, they all mean the same site).

LEVELS

An atom may contain up to seven levels.

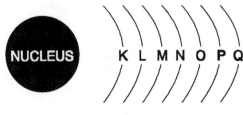

NUCLEUS   K L M N O P Q

Naturally, these levels exist only if there are electrons present at that level.

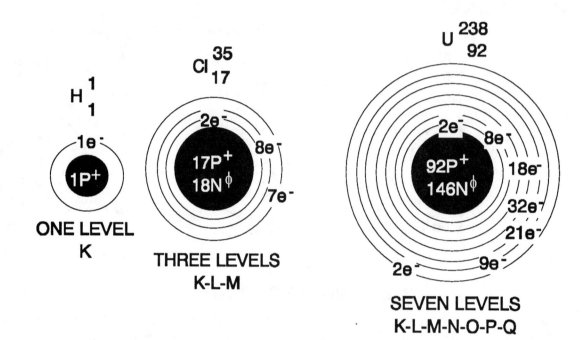

CONSTRUCTING ATOMS

Given the following information we can construct a model of an atom.

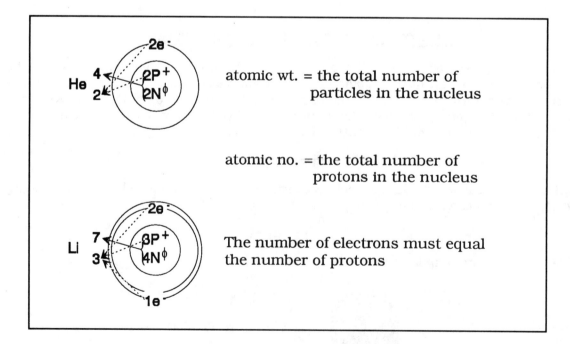

atomic wt. = the total number of particles in the nucleus

atomic no. = the total number of protons in the nucleus

The number of electrons must equal the number of protons

Number of Elements

There are 104 recognized elements at the present time. Ninety-two (92) of these are naturally occurring and twelve (12) are synthetic (man-made).

CHEMICAL SYMBOLS

Each element has its own chemical symbol. This symbol may be one capital letter or a capital letter followed by a lower case letter.

EXAMPLE:

H = hydrogen

He = helium

C = carbon

Ca = calcium

Here is a list of common chemical symbols that you might be expected to know for the CLEP Examination.

CHEMICAL SYMBOL	ELEMENT	CHEMICAL SYMBOL	ELEMENT
1. Al	Aluminum	11. Na	Sodium
2. Ca	Calcium	12. S	Sulfur
3. C	Carbon	13. U	Uranium
4. Cu	Copper	14. Zn	Zinc
5. Fe	Iron	15. Hg	Mercury
6. Pb	Lead	16. Br	Bromine
7. Mg	Magnesium	17. N_2	Nitrogen
8. P	Phosphorus	18. O_2	Oxygen
9. K	Potassium	19. H_2	Hydrogen
10. Si	Silicon	20. Cl_2	Chlorine

Numbers 1-14 exist naturally as solids; 15 and 16 exist as liquids. Numbers 17-20 normally exist as diatomic gases.

Diatomic Molecules

Diatomic molecules are made when two atoms form one molecule.

The diatomic gases have a "2" **subscript** written to the lower right of the chemical symbol (O_2, H_2, N_2, and Cl_2).

These gases exist in their free state as pairs of atoms and are referred to as **diatomic molecules** (two atoms forming one molecule).

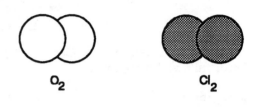

O_2 Cl_2

COMPOUNDS

Given the right circumstances, elements, compounds, or both may react with each other to form new products. The products formed may be compounds or released elements and will have their own special chemical and physical properties.

CHEMICAL REACTIONS

A chemical reaction is the process by which elements and compounds split or combine to form different elements and compounds.

TWO ELEMENTS

	hydrogen + oxygen → H_2 + O_2 →	water H_2O (unbalanced)
Physical Properties:	gas, odorless, tasteless, colorless	liquid, odorless, tasteless, colorless
Chemical Properties:	very explosive, supports combustion	**Not** explosive and does **not** support combustion

TWO COMPOUNDS

Sodium hydroxide	+	hydrochloric acid	→	Sodium chloride	+	water
Na (OH)	+	HCl	→	NaCl	+	H_2O
BASE	+	ACID	→	SALT	+	WATER

NOTE: an acid + a base combine to form a salt and water. (OH) with or without brackets, usually denotes a **base**. H beginning a chemical equation usually denotes an **acid**.

COMPOUND AND AN ELEMENT

Sodium Chloride	+	Fluorine	→	Sodium fluoride	+	Chlorine
NaCl	+	F_2	→	NaF	+	Cl_2 (unbalanced)

LAW OF CONSERVATION OF MATTER

At this point, it would be wise to recall the **Law of Conservation of Matter.** Simply stated: matter can neither be created nor destroyed.

On the previous page is the reaction formula, $H_2 + O_2 \rightarrow H_2O$. It is true that hydrogen and oxygen combine to form water. However, the **correct amount** of H_2 must combine with the **correct amount** of O_2 in order to produce H_2O.

The "**correct**" amount of **reactants** in a reaction (the ingredients are called reactants) is the least amount that allows the reaction to proceed.

H_2O is the proper formula for water. H_2 and O_2 is the proper way to represent the reactants. Unfortunately, in the overall formula there is **no** equality.

H_2 = two atoms of hydrogen (one molecule)

O_2 = two atoms of oxygen (one molecule)

H_2O = two atoms hydrogen, one atom oxygen (one molecule)

$$H_2 + O_2 \quad \rightarrow \quad H_2O$$
$$2 + 2 \quad \rightarrow \quad 2 + 1$$

In the reaction as written, one oxygen has been "lost". Our Law of Conservation of Matter states that this cannot happen. In order to remedy the situation and comply with the Law, a balance must be struck on each side of the arrow.

Suppose we use two molecules of H_2 (four atoms) on the lefthand side of the arrow and two molecules of water on the right-hand side of the arrow. This **balances** our formula—the amount of matter on right side of the arrow equals the amount of matter on the left side of the arrow:

$$\underline{2}\,H_2 \quad + \quad O_2 \quad \rightarrow \quad \underline{2}\,H_2O$$
$$4 \quad + \quad 2 \qquad 4 + 2$$

Another example is the $NaCl + F_2 \rightarrow NaF + Cl_2$.

As we see above, the matter to the left of the arrow is **not** equal to the matter to the right of the arrow. By adjusting the number of molecules of the reactants, or products, the least amount of matter needed in this reaction can be determined:

$$2NaCl + F_2 \rightarrow 2NaF + Cl_2$$

Notice, too, the atoms to the left of the arrow are the same as the atoms to the right of the arrow. At no time can we begin with some matter and not see it again after the chemical reaction. All ingredients must appear in the products. By the same reasoning, atoms cannot just appear in the products if they were not part of the reactants.

Bonding

Compounds form in two distinct ways—covalently and ionically.

COVALENT BONDING

When matter combines chemically in a covalent bond, it **shares** electrons. Covalent means sharing.

EXAMPLE: $2H_2 + O_2 \rightarrow 2H_2O$ 4 H + 2 O_x will produce 2 molecules of H_2O

EACH HYDROGEN SHARES ITS ELECTRON WITH THE OTHER HYDROGEN

EACH OXYGEN SHARES TWO ELECTRONS WITH THE OTHER OXYGEN

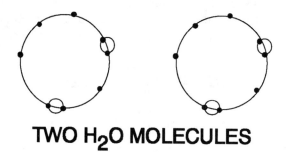

TWO H₂O MOLECULES

The two diatomic molecules of hydrogen combine with the one diatomic molecule of oxygen. During the reaction, the diatomic molecules of hydrogen and oxygen are broken apart and reassembled.

IONIC BONDING

Another kind of chemical bonding is the **ionic bond**. In this type of bond the electrons are moved from one atom to another. Therefore, an ionic bond is one in which an atom gains or loses an electron.

EXAMPLE: $2 Na + Cl_2 \rightarrow 2 Na Cl$

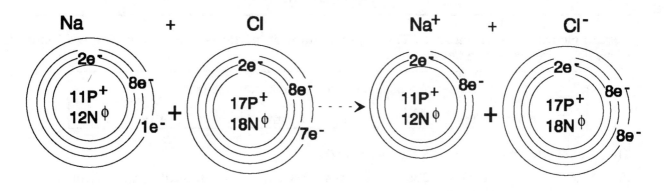

Na^+ and Cl^- can be written with "+" and "-" indicating they are charged (electrically **un**balanced). They are now called **ions** because they no longer fit the definition of an atom.

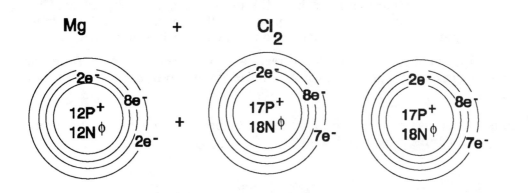

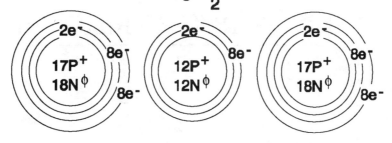

Radioactivity

Certain elements decay naturally. That is, they throw off particles and energy. The two kinds of particles are **alpha** and **beta**:

α—alpha particle = He_2^4 (a helium nucleus)

β—beta particle = e^- [from the decay of a neutron ($n^\varnothing = p^+ + e^- +$ neutrino)]

The form of energy produced is a **gamma** ray (Υ).

EXAMPLE: In the decay of U238, a and b particles are thrown off until a stable form of lead (Pb) is produced.

$$U_{92}^{238} \xrightarrow{\alpha} Th_{90}^{234} \xrightarrow{\beta} Pa_{91}^{234}$$

$$U_{92}^{238}$$
$$- \alpha_2^4$$
$$\overline{}$$
$$Th_{90}^{234}$$

beta decay = loss of an e^- from the ($p^+ + e^- +$ neutrino) neutron. This leaves a p^+ in the neucleus in place of a $N^\varnothing$. No change in the number of particles (at.wt.) but a gain of one p^+. Only Pa has at.no. 91.

To simplify, an alpha decay results in the loss of 4 amu from the atomic weight and a loss of 2 from the atomic number.

A beta decay results in the loss of a neutron but a gain in proton. That means **No** loss in atomic weight but a gain of 1 in atomic number.

DECAY OF U^{238}:

$$U_{92}^{238} \xrightarrow{\alpha} Th_{90}^{234} \xrightarrow{\beta} Pa_{91}^{234} \xrightarrow{\beta} U_{92}^{234}$$

$$\xrightarrow{\alpha}$$

$$Th_{90}^{230} \xrightarrow{\alpha} Ra_{88}^{226} \xrightarrow{\alpha} Rn_{86}^{222} \xrightarrow{\beta} Po_{84}^{218}$$

$$\xrightarrow{\alpha}$$

$$\xrightarrow{\alpha} Ti_{81}^{210} \xrightarrow{\beta}$$

$$Pb_{82}^{214} \xrightarrow{\beta} Bi_{83}^{214} \updownarrow \qquad \qquad Pb_{82}^{210}$$

$$\xrightarrow{\beta}$$

$$\xrightarrow{\beta} Po_{84}^{214} \xrightarrow{\alpha}$$

$$Bi_{83}^{210} \xrightarrow{\beta} Po_{84}^{210} \xrightarrow{\alpha} Pb_{82}^{206}$$

It is possible to determine the rate of decay of the radioactive elements. Knowing the percentages of radioactive elements in a rock and the rate of decay of those elements, it is possible to determine the "age" of the rock (dating).

HALF LIFE

The half-life of a radioactive substance is the amount of time it takes for one-half of that substance to undergo decay. For example: U^{238} has a half-life of 4.5 billion years. This means that if one pound of U^{238} existed 4.5 billion years ago, only half of the original U^{238} would exist today. The other half would have decayed into the daughter elements (Th, Ra, Rn, etc.) and Pb^{206}.

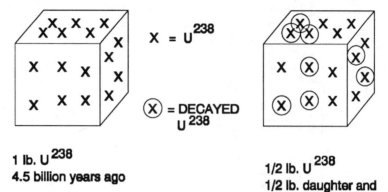

X = U^{238}

$\boxed{X}$ = DECAYED U^{238}

1 lb. U^{238}
4.5 billion years ago

1/2 lb. U^{238}
1/2 lb. daughter and
stable elements now

In order to calculate the amount of original radioactive elements remaining after a number of half-lives, one must follow the formula: $\left(\frac{1}{2}\right)^{n}$.

EXAMPLE: A substance passed through 4 half-lives. How much of the original substance remains? How much has decayed?

$$\left(\tfrac{1}{2}\right)^{n} = \left(\tfrac{1}{2}\right)^{4} = \tfrac{1}{2} \times \tfrac{1}{2} \times \tfrac{1}{2} \times \tfrac{1}{2} = \tfrac{1}{16}$$

Then only $\frac{1}{16}$ of the original radioactive substance remains, and $\frac{15}{16}$ has decayed ($\frac{1}{16} + \frac{15}{16} = \frac{16}{16}$ or the whole amount).

EXAMPLE: A radioactive substance has a half-life of 25 years and passes through 5 half-lives.

(a) How many years does it take to pass through 5 half-lives?

(b) How much of the original material remains?

(c) How many years will it be before 99% of the original substance decays?

ANSWERS: (a) $\dfrac{25 \text{ years}}{1 \text{ half life}} \times 5 \text{ half lives} = 125 \text{ years}$

(b) $\left(\dfrac{1}{2}\right)^n = \left(\dfrac{1}{2}\right)^5 = \dfrac{1}{2} \times \dfrac{1}{2} \times \dfrac{1}{2} \times \dfrac{1}{2} \times \dfrac{1}{2} = \dfrac{1}{32}$ of the original substance remains

(c) $\left(\dfrac{1}{2}\right)^n = \left(\dfrac{1}{2}\right)^2 = \dfrac{1}{4}$

$\left(\dfrac{1}{2}\right)^3 = \dfrac{1}{8}$

$\left(\dfrac{1}{2}\right)^4 = \dfrac{1}{16}$

$\left(\dfrac{1}{2}\right)^5 = \dfrac{1}{32}$

$\left(\dfrac{1}{2}\right)^6 = \dfrac{1}{64}$

$\left(\dfrac{1}{2}\right)^7 = \dfrac{1}{128}$

$\dfrac{1}{128}$ is closer to $\dfrac{1}{100}$ (1% original substance remaining, 99% decayed) than $\dfrac{1}{64}$. So, the substance must pass through close to seven half-lives.

Earth Science Review

The Earth Sciences cover a number of areas. In this review, astronomy and total earth structure and composition are included.

Astronomy

UNIVERSE

The universe is all of the observable space surrounding the earth. Most of this space is empty. However, pockets of matter and energy do exist within this emptiness.

The matter of the universe consists of all known naturally occurring elements. These elements may exist alone or in combination with other elements. In many instances, elemental matter is further reduced into sub-atomic particles such as protons, electrons or neutrons.

If the matter within some of these "pockets" combines in response to gravitational attraction, different astronomical "bodies" may form. A list of some of these "bodies" includes:

Smallest

METEOR - is a luminous streak of light which occurs when a meteoroid (small piece of interplanetary material) rapidly enters the earth's atmosphere causing atmospheric frictional heating.

COMET - a small icy and dusty object (the nucleus) that becomes visible as a glowing, diffuse coma and tail which form during its near approach to the sun.

PLANETOIDS - thought to be left over from creation of solar system—they are smaller than planets.

SATELLITES - any object that is in orbit around another object, usually a planet.

PLANETS - the largest bodies that revolve around stars.

STARS - gaseous bodies that give off energy and revolve around their galactic center.

NEBULA - any diffuse astronomical object, such as a **planetary nebula** (remnant of the atmosphere of a dying star), **extragalactic nebula** and **emission nebula** (a type of interstellar gas cloud).

GALAXIES - collections of billions of stars revolving around some common center.

Largest

The detectable energy of the universe results from the rearrangement or destruction of matter. Some forms of detectable energy are radio waves, light waves, ultra-violet waves, infra-red waves and X-rays. We gather our knowledge about the universe from the many forms of energy that reach the earth.

The size of the universe is huge—some 16-20 billion light years in diameter. Because of its size, it is sometimes better to think of the universe as made up of two parts:

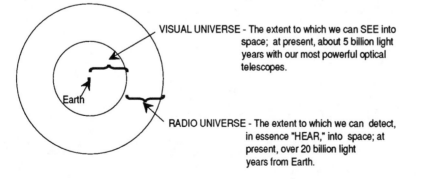

VISUAL UNIVERSE - The extent to which we can SEE into space; at present, about 5 billion light years with our most powerful optical telescopes.

RADIO UNIVERSE - The extent to which we can detect, in essence "HEAR," into space; at present, over 20 billion light years from Earth.

42

LIGHT YEAR

Distances in space outside our solar system are measured in units called light years. A **light year** is the **distance** light travels in one year. To calculate the value of a light year, one must know that light travels 186,000 miles in one second. Remember these two important facts for the examination: the speed of light is 186,000 mi./sec., and a light year is approximately 6 trillion miles (distance unit).

TOOLS OF THE ASTRONOMER

OPTICAL TELESCOPES

In 1609, Galileo constructed the first **refractor** telescope. Prior to Galileo, man had only his eyes to view the sky. This invention opened new vistas into a very old science.

The refracting telescope uses lenses to **bend** light waves. Eyeglasses do the same thing!

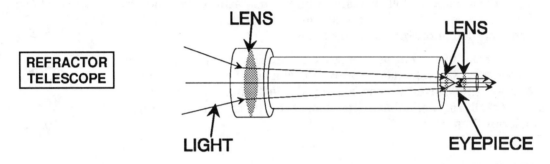

The light from stars or other heavenly bodies passes through the large lens and is bent. This concentrates the light near the eyepiece. By adjusting the eyepiece, light can be focused so that the view is a relatively bright image of the body.

Galileo's invention allowed him to become the first person to view Saturn's rings, the moons of Jupiter, and the craters on the moon.

Sir Isaac Newton (b. 1642) invented the **reflector** telescope. As the name implies, a mirror is the key ingredient in this instrument.

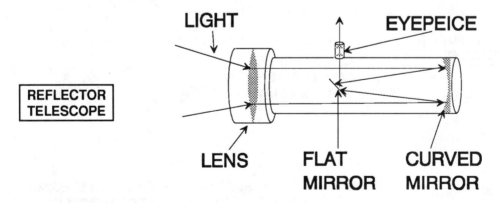

As we see from the above diagram, light from some source travels down the tube to a curved (parabolic) mirror. The light is reflected from the mirror. Due to the curvature, the light is concentrated at the flat mirror, where it is reflected to the eyepiece. The eyepiece is adjustable so that the light may be focused and the image viewed clearly.

43

The reflector telescopes are the largest of the optical instruments. A reflector of a 200" mirror is located at the Hale Observatory, Mt. Palomar, California. The former U.S.S.R. also had a large reflector measuring some 236" in diameter. However, it is so heavy that it sags under its own weight and renders the telescope less than perfect. We now have a monolithic mirrored telescope that is 250" in diameter. The multi-mirrored telescopes can be made even bigger than that.

The Yerkes Observatory in Wisconsin owns a 40" lens telescope. Refractors are limited in size to 40" in diameter. If made larger than 40", they sag and take on a "pear" or "tear-drop" shape.

Generally speaking, the larger the lens or mirror, the greater the light gathering power of the telescope.

Both the size and the cost of optical instruments are necessarily limited. Fortunately, the addition of a camera to either one of these instruments broadens its capability. The film in the camera can perform a feat even the human eye cannot do—that is, fix an image of a light source viewed for minutes, or, if need be, hours.

By driving the telescope to follow a star's apparent path across the sky and holding the lens of the camera open for long periods of time, faint light can be recorded and examined **any time**.

To this end, special films that are sensitive to certain wavelengths (infra-red, ultra-violet, X-rays) have been developed to gain different perspectives of the universe. These special films must be flown (via balloons or satellites) well above the denser parts of our atmosphere which block out these rays.

Special filters and cameras are added to reflecting telescopes to build a Schmidt telescope. They are used for color photography of the universe.

SCHMIDT TELESCOPE

CAMERA FOR A PERMANENT RECORD

CLOCK DRIVE TO COMPENSATE FOR THE EARTH'S ROTATION

THE LENSES ARE COATED WITH A SPECIAL FILM TO ELIMINATE MOST OF THE COLOR DISTORTION THAT IS CAUSED BY THE LIGHT TRAVELING FROM THE AIR TO GLASS AND BACK TO THE AIR

Satellites have been used as observatories in space. The Skylab project had a daily observation period devoted to solar and earth observation. The Hubble space telescope, even with its flawed mirrors, gives the best pictures of our universe yet, after the data is run through a computer.

The greatest advantage space observatories have over any Earth-based observatory is that they do **not** have to look through an atmosphere which can diffuse and absorb radiation.

SPECTROSCOPE

Finally, but no less important than the preceding optical instruments, there is the **spectroscope**. The principle by which the spectroscope operates is refraction. Light passes through a tube with lenses. The lens bends the light, causing it to concentrate into a narrow beam. The light is then passed through a prism or diffraction grating where it is separated into the colors red, orange, yellow, green, blue, indigo and violet.

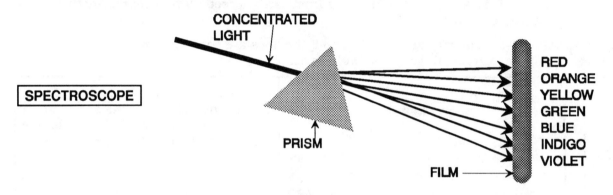

The light from stars can be compared to light originating here on earth. The light is recorded on film by a spectrograph. The film has guide numbers known as Angstrom units (A = 10^{-8} cm or 10^{-10} m). Visible light has a measure of 3500 to 7000 angstroms.

It is known that certain elements will glow when heated. The light given off is like the name of the element—it does **not** change. Therefore, by studying light from a star and seeing these characteristic color prints, one can determine the composition of the star. On Earth, for example, sodium gives off a characteristic yellow light when it is heated. Most elements and compounds have been "tagged" (finger-printed) so that determining the composition of stars near and far is a relatively easy task.

The spectroscope can also determine the speed of an object in space relative to the earth. This particular phenomenom is known as the **Doppler Shift**. You have probably noticed this effect if a train, plane or truck passed you moving at a relatively fast speed. The **sound** (pitch) of the vehicle moving toward you is higher than the sound of the same vehicle as it passes and moves away from you.

All that happens in this situation is that sound waves compress somewhat as the vehicle moves toward you (source moving in the same direction as the wave) and stretch out as the vehicle moves away from you (source moving in the opposite direction from the wave).

This very same principle applies to light waves. If the source is moving **toward** earth, a **"blue-shift"** will occur. If the source is moving **away** from earth, a **"red shift"** occurs. Another name for this is the **Doppler shift**.

Again using Na (sodium) with its yellow lines—if the lines are compared to an earth-based Na source, one of the following three cases would develop:

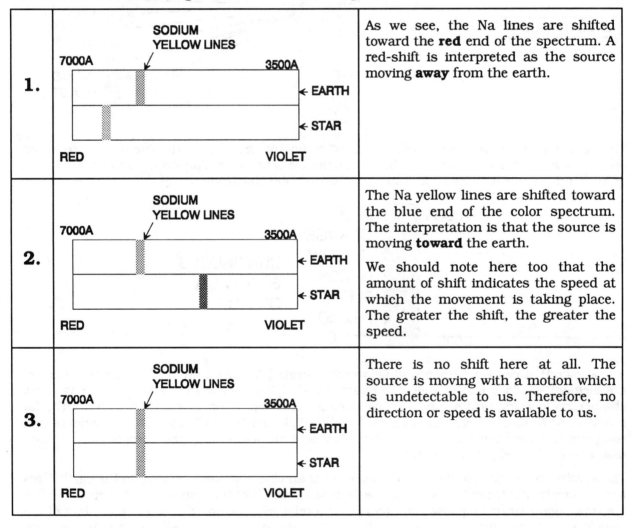

1.	SODIUM YELLOW LINES; 7000A ... 3500A; ← EARTH; ← STAR; RED ... VIOLET	As we see, the Na lines are shifted toward the **red** end of the spectrum. A red-shift is interpreted as the source moving **away** from the earth.
2.	SODIUM YELLOW LINES; 7000A ... 3500A; ← EARTH; ← STAR; RED ... VIOLET	The Na yellow lines are shifted toward the blue end of the color spectrum. The interpretation is that the source is moving **toward** the earth. We should note here too that the amount of shift indicates the speed at which the movement is taking place. The greater the shift, the greater the speed.
3.	SODIUM YELLOW LINES; 7000A ... 3500A; ← EARTH; ← STAR; RED ... VIOLET	There is no shift here at all. The source is moving with a motion which is undetectable to us. Therefore, no direction or speed is available to us.

RADIO TELESCOPE

In 1931, Karl Jansky discovered another use for the relatively new invention called the radio. He was hired by a telephone company to discover why their overseas cables had poor transmitting properties at certain times.

Jansky set up a small antenna and radio at the Jersey shore. He discovered that the cause of the garbled transmissions was the sun. Each day from sunrise till sunset, static filled the radio wave lengths he monitored. After sunset, the static decreased to a reasonable level which did not distort transmissions.

Jansky's use of the radio telescope has broadened since 1931. Today, antennas as large as 18.5 acres (Arecibo, Puerto Rico), and 250' in diameter (Jodrell Bank, England) are in use to gather more information about the universe.

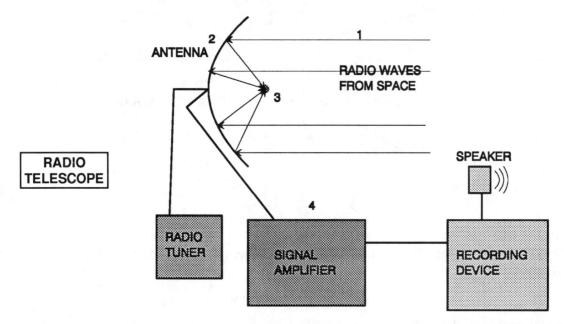

Generally speaking, the radio telescope works in this fashion: The radio waves from the source are gathered by the antenna and reflected to a collector. The collected waves are transmitted to an amplifier where they are strengthened; and from there, they go to the recording device.

Perhaps the most important discovery made by radio astronomers has been the **QUASAR (Quasi-Stellar Radio Source)**. It is thought by some astronomers that **QUASARS** originated some 20 billion years ago—a few billion years after the birth of our universe.

COSMOLOGY

Scientists involved with trying to determine the origin of our universe are called cosmologists. To date, three major theories have been proposed as to how our universe came into being.

STEADY—STATE THEORY

The Steady-State Theory states that there is a central point in the universe. Around this point, H_2 gas is created. The H_2 gas, in turn, creates galaxies. These galaxies move away from this central point, thereby creating a space in which newly created H_2 can form a new galaxy.

The continuation of creating H_2 and H_2 creating galaxies and galaxies moving away from the central point, has always been in existence and is **not** subject to time. In other words, this pattern has always existed and **will** always exist.

Obviously, the idea that something can "always be" is not easy to comprehend. Our experience leads us to believe that **change** is the rule and **not** the exception.

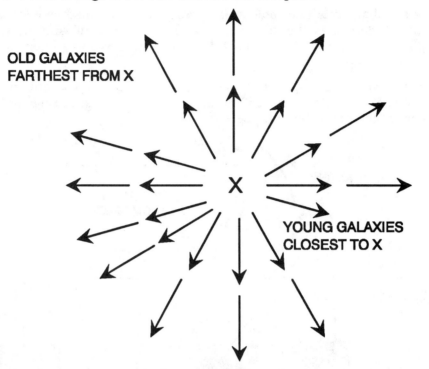

OLD GALAXIES
FARTHEST FROM X

X

YOUNG GALAXIES
CLOSEST TO X

Another problem with this theory is that the H_2 gas is being created from nothing. That's really hard to understand.

BIG BANG THEORY

The Big Bang theory holds that at some time in the past, all the matter was at one central spot in the universe. This matter became very unstable and an explosion occurred. The bits of matter became galaxies and spread out into space.

All matter in the universe
collected in one central
location. This matter is
(or becomes) unstable

A huge explosion occurs
and matter moves away
from the central location

→   Galaxies
     formed

The data supporting this theory is: 1) most of the galaxies observed are moving apart much like an exploded aerial bomb; 2) it supplies an origin for the energy needed to move these galaxies through space.

OSCILLATING/PULSATING/EXPANSION-CONTRACTION THEORY

In this theory, a "big bang" is the origin of the universe. However, the galaxies travel out into space and then begin to decelerate. At some point in time, the galaxies stop and begin to fall back into some common center due to their gravitational attraction. When all the matter reaches that point it will smash together and explode again like a Big Bang.

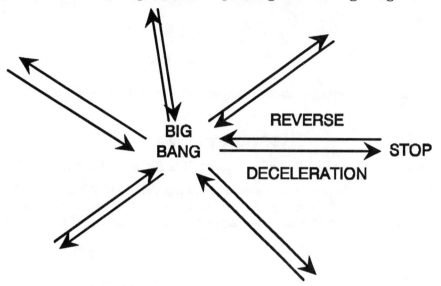

Studies are now being made to determine if there is enough matter in the universe to create enough gravitation to cause this pulsating universe to exist. Enough matter could allow a pulsating universe; and if there is too little matter, the Big Bang is likely the best explanation of the present-day universe.

MATTER IN THE UNIVERSE

GALAXIES

Galaxies are clusters of millions and/or billions of stars. One of the more interesting facts about galaxies is their shape.

Our own galaxy, called the **Milky Way**, has at least 2 spiral arms. Note too, the diameter is 100,000 light years wide. This makes the Milky Way Galaxy rather large compared to anything but the universe or other galaxies.

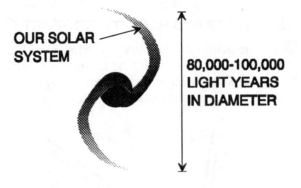

OUR SOLAR SYSTEM

80,000-100,000 LIGHT YEARS IN DIAMETER

We (the solar system) are located about three-fifths out from the center of the Milky Way Galaxy.

SOLAR SYSTEM

Our place in the universe is called the solar system. It is named after our star SOL (the sun).

The sun and the members of the solar system probably originated from a gas cloud (nebula) which contracted around itself, creating rotation and gravity. This particular theory of creation (there are many) is called the **Protoplanet Hypothesis**. It was developed by Weiszacker in 1944.

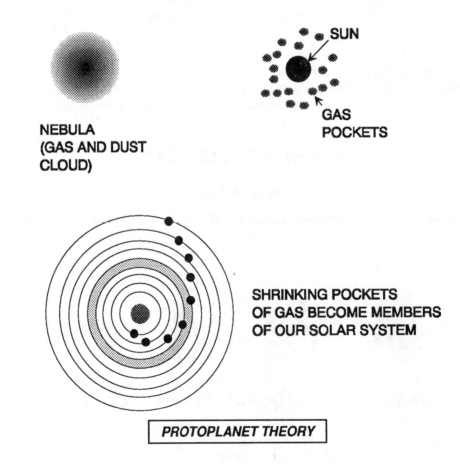

NEBULA (GAS AND DUST CLOUD)

SUN

GAS POCKETS

SHRINKING POCKETS OF GAS BECOME MEMBERS OF OUR SOLAR SYSTEM

PROTOPLANET THEORY

As the cloud shrinks and rotation occurs, eddies are formed by the friction of matter piling up against itself. These eddies eventually form planets, moons, comets, meteors and asteroids (planetoids).

Most of the cloud forms the sun. All the contracting matter slams together, creating a tremendous temperature rise to somewhere in excess of 24,000,000°F. This is important because high temperatures are needed to create **thermonuclear reactions**.

The composition of the sun is mostly atomic hydrogen (H) gas. The H reacts with other H to form He. Some matter is lost:

4 H atoms combine to make one He atom.

The matter that is lost is converted into energy. However, we must realize that billions of these reactions are occurring every second.

Einstein's equation: $E = mc^2$

E = energy
m = mass (matter lost)
c^2 = speed of light × speed of light
Thus, $E = m \cdot 186,000/sec. \cdot 186,000/sec.$ = (large number bigger than billions)

You can easily see that E will equal a fantastically large number which represents the energy produced in just **one** second!

The sun has been producing this energy for at least 5 billion years and will continue to do so for about 5 billion more.

THE SUN'S STRUCTURE AND COMPOSITION

The sun has an interior which is extremely hot (24 million°F). At the surface of the sun is the **photosphere**. This is the part of the sun where light emerges from the interior. Temperature at the surface is approximately 10,000°F or 6,000°C.

Sunspots are seen on the surface of the sun. They are cooler (but are still very hot!) than the surrounding areas and therefore appear as dark spots.

The atmosphere of the sun is divided into two parts: the chromosphere and the corona. Both may be observed during a total eclipse of the sun or by using a **coronagraph** (special attachment for a telescope). Features such as solar flares and solar prominences exist in these layers.

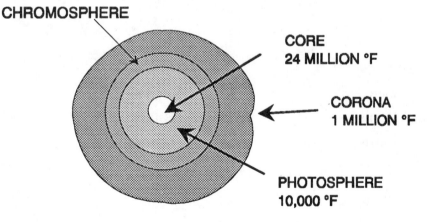

The sun is 846,000 miles in diameter and rotates once (at the equator) every 25 days.

THE PLANETS

There are nine planets in the solar system. Each one, because of its distance from the sun and its size, has its own special characteristics. The planets follow elliptical orbits around the sun.

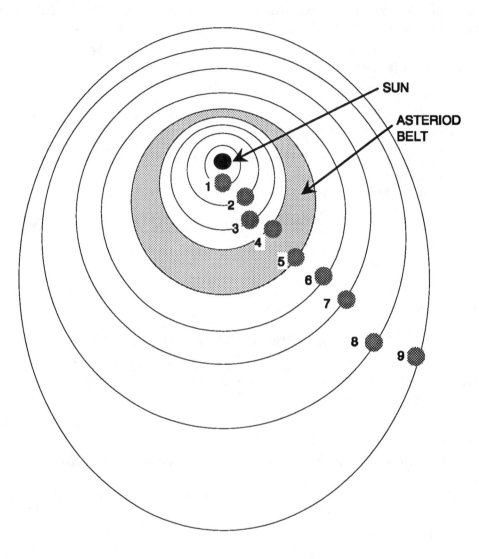

INNER PLANETS:

1. Mercury
2. Venus
3. Earth
4. Mars

OUTER PLANETS:

5. Jupiter
6. Saturn
7. Uranus
8. Neptune
9. Pluto

The force of gravity and the planet's motion hold the planets in orbit around the sun.

The planets are listed below in the order of distance from the sun outward into space:

MERCURY

1. the warmest planet
2. the closest planet to the sun
3. no satellites (moons)
4. no atmosphere
5. slow rotation

VENUS

1. about the same size as Earth
2. very warm (900°F—hot enough to melt lead)
3. no satellites
4. atmospheric composition: CO_2, H_2O?, H_2SO_4?
5. rotates in opposite direction from all the other planets (retrograde rotation East to West)

Venus has a very dense atmosphere solid with clouds. With probes we have been able to see the actual surface of Venus, showing it has spreading rift zones, old lava flows, ridges, bright parallel lines, etc. The dense clouds and atmosphere keep Venus' temperature very hot because of the "**greenhouse effect**".

GREENHOUSE EFFECT

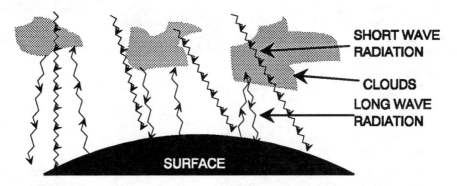

SHORT WAVE RADIATION

CLOUDS

LONG WAVE RADIATION

SURFACE

Short wave radiation from the sun enters Venus' atmosphere and may be absorbed in the clouds or at the surface. This radiation (heat) can be re-radiated, but only as long-wave radiation. Long waves are easily bounced around in the atmosphere (absorbed-released, absorbed-released, etc.) by the CO_2 and/or H_2O and/or H_2S_4 in the clouds. This is called the "greenhouse effect" because of the similarity and function of the clouds as compared to the glass of a greenhouse.

THE EARTH

1. located at perfect position from sun, allowing H_2O to exist in all three physical states (solid, liquid, gas). Average distance from the sun is 93 million miles.
2. one satellite called **moon**
   a) moon located 243,000 mi. from Earth
   b) moon is the main cause of tides (the sun contributes about 30% to tidal movement))
3. atmosphere of Earth is unique—it is composed 78% of N_2 and 21% of O_2

MARS (THE RED PLANET)

1. half the size of Earth
2. thin atmosphere composed of CO_2, N_2, H_2O
3. shows seasonal changes
4. has ice caps at polar regions
5. has "weather" (huge dust storms)
6. has two large moons
   a) Deimos
   b) Phobos

THE ASTEROID BELT

Located between Mars and Jupiter is a bed of rock particles ranging from sand size diameter up to 250 miles in diameter (**Ceres**).

Scientists are not sure why these rocks are here. Speculation includes a planet which broke apart because of opposing tidal forces, or the asteroids may be the remains of 2 planetoids which collided causing both to break apart, or they may be a planet that never quite formed.

JUPITER

1. the largest planet (88 thousand miles diameter)
2. has at least 16 satellites
3. has a red spot in its atmosphere
4. very fast rotation (10 hours and 50 minutes/1 rot)—this causes planet to flatten at poles and bulge at equator
5. atmospheric composition: H_2, CH_4, NH_3

SATURN

1. second largest planet
2. has band of rings moving around its equator
   a) the rings consist of hundreds of ringlets
   b) thickness of rings not over 10 miles
3. atmospheric composition: CH_4, H_2, NH_3
4. has at least 27 satellites

URANUS AND NEPTUNE

1. about the same size (27.5 - 25.5 thousand miles in diameter)
2. number of satellites:
   a) Uranus—at least fifteen satellites (also has at least 9 rings)
   b) Neptune—two known satellites at the present time (the outermost planet until 1999)
3. atmospheric composition: CH_4 and H_2

PLUTO

1. the smallest planet with a diameter of 1,612 miles
2. Pluto is the farthest planet from the sun most of the time (4 billion miles) and may be a captured asteroid
3. has a moon called Charon
4. does not orbit in the same plane as the rest of the planets

The Earth

About 4,500,000,000 years ago, the Earth finished its protoplanet phase. The young planet's internal structure and composition was probably much like it is today.

Although man has drilled into and investigated only the crust (lithosphere) of the Earth, much about the internal structure is known from indirect evidence.

EARTH'S STRUCTURE

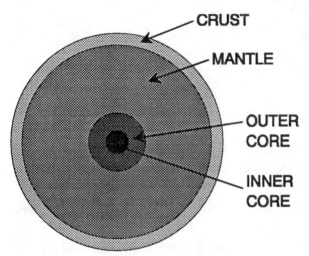

The inner core is thought to be made of Fe and Ni existing in a **solid** state.

The outer core is composed of Fe and Ni existing in a **liquid** state.

The **mantle** is composed largely of Fe and Ni near the outer core and of stone (Fe, Mg silicates) as it approaches the crust.

The crust, or lithosphere, is separated from the mantle by the MOHO discontinuity. It is composed of silicates which are further separated according to density and composition.

Crustal minerals making up continents form granitoid rocks heavy in Silica and Al (Aluminum)—called **SIAL** for short.

The other kind of crustal mineral (basalt) forms the ocean floor and is referred to as **SIMA**— Silica, Fe (Iron), and Mg (Magnesium).

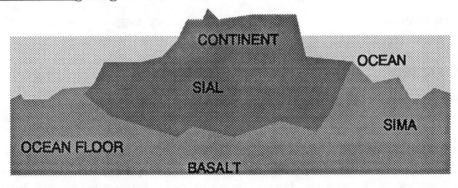

Information about the earth's interior composition is largely acquired by studying meteorites. It is assumed that the mineral composition of meteorites is the same as that of the Earth because they had a common beginning.

Information about the structure of the Earth's interior comes from the study of earthquakes **(seismology)**.

Waves generated by earthquakes often travel through the entire Earth. These waves (P and S), act differently as they pass through layers of the earth.

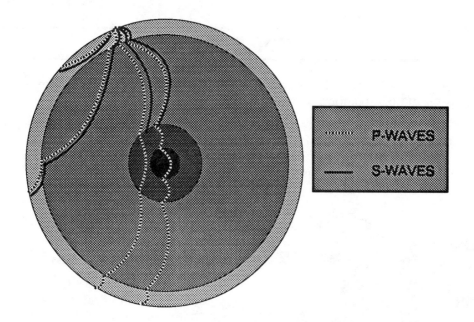

P-waves (primary waves) travel through the entire Earth. Each time they enter into a deeper layer (medium) they are refracted (bent). They just about slow down and then resume their journey at speeds exceeding those in the upper layers.

The refraction and speed change indicates to scientists that the earth has different layers (crust, outer core, inner core, mantle).

Notice in the diagram that **S-waves** (secondary waves) are different from P-waves. P-waves are compressional; that is, the energy travels in the same direction as the motion of the atoms and molecules.

P-WAVE
COMPRESSIONAL

ENERGY →
← MOTION →

S-WAVES
TRANSVERSAL

ENERGY ——→   MOTION (up/down)

S-waves are **transverse** waves. That is, the energy and the motion are at right angles to one another. A transverse wave cannot travel through a liquid. This can be tested at the surface. The fact that S-waves do not always arrive at seismological stations leads scientists to believe the outer core is liquid.

THE SURFACE OF THE EARTH

The Earth's surface is constantly changing. On the large scale, changes occur because of destructive forces acting on surface rocks. Radioactivity within the earth causes rocks deep within the lower crust and upper mantle to melt. This liquid rock is less dense than surrounding solid rock, so it rises towards the surface. Although scientists cannot trace all the steps, they believe the rising rock is one part of a huge magma/rock convection cell.

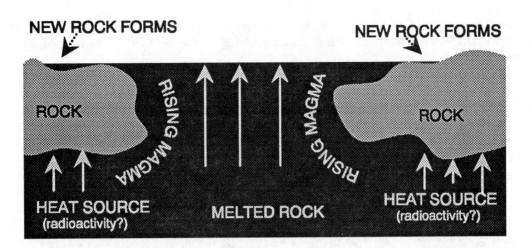

The rising liquid rock, called **magma**, makes its way to the surface to places we call **mid-ocean ridges**. These ridges are usually on the ocean floor. Oceanographic mapping by boat and satellite shows these ridges are connected and form an underwater mountain chain 40,000 miles in length on the ocean floor. Occasionally ocean mountains break the surface. Two examples are Iceland and the Azores.

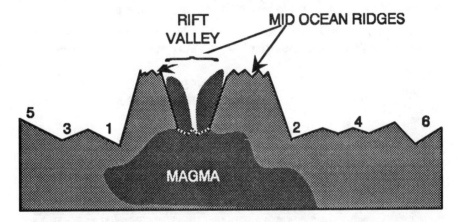

New magma forces the old ridges to move apart and form a **rift-valley**. This magma displaces the older rock and solidifies. As more new magma is injected into the ridges, more displacement occurs. Mid-ocean ridges are regions of frequent earthquakes (rock displacement).

In this manner, the sea floor is spreading away from the area of the mid-ocean ridges. A study of the rocks at numbers 1 and 2 shows that fossils found in the sediments are younger than in numbers 3 and 4 and numbers 5 and 6. Also, the thickness of sediments is less at 1 and 2 compared to the others.

One interpretation of the above is that numbers 1 and 2 were not present when the animals and plants that formed the fossils were alive; also, that the thickness of sediments depends largely upon time. The longer the rocks were there, the thicker the sediments deposited upon them.

As the sea floor spreads away from the ridges, they carry or push the continents. An example is the North American continent being pushed along by the sea floor originating at the **Mid-Atlantic** ridge.

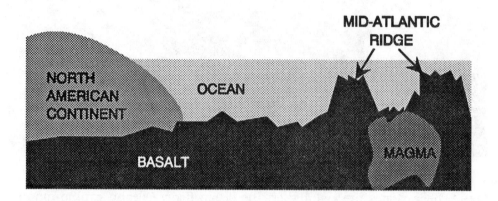

That part of the ridge, sea-floor, and North American continent, all belong to what scientists call a **plate**. The plate is known as the North American plate. There are at least five major plates and many minor plates which make up the crust of the earth.

Plates often collide with each other, resulting in severe earthquakes and vulcanism. The Pacific plate striking the European-Asian plate is, perhaps, the best understood collision at present.

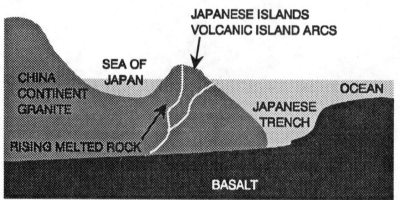

The Pacific plate encounters the European-Asian plate, and the sea-floor is forced beneath the continental rocks. This forms a deep ocean trench.

As the sea-floor subsides, it begins to heat quickly because of burial and friction. Some crustal material begins melting. Since there are numerous earth movements causing cracks in the overlying rock, the melted rock material seeps upward toward the sea-floor of the European-Asian plate.

Magma oozing out on to the surface of the sea floor, forms many volcanoes. Those large enough to survive to the sea surface eventually formed the Japanese Islands.

Other areas of crustal movement and/or volcanoes include the Aegean (Mediterranean), India, Himalayas, California (earthquakes), and Alaska (earthquakes).

The whole idea that the continents are moving was first expressed by Wegener in 1915. His hypothesis was known as the Continental Drift Theory. At present, the theory is known as **plate tectonics**.

ROCKS

Rocks are classified according to their texture, composition and origin.

IGNEOUS ROCKS

Igneous rocks form from melted rock minerals. Magma (melted rock **below** the surface) forms intrusive igneous rocks such as granite, felsite, gabbro and diabase.

Because the magma is located below the surface, it cools slowly, forming a coarse-textured rock with large mineral crystals and/or grains. Again, because these rocks form **below the surface**, they are called **intrusive igneous** rocks.

Lava (the melted rock that reaches the surface) forms **extrusive igneous** rocks such as basalt, pumice, obsidian. Little or no crystals or grains are present on these rocks because the lava cools so quickly. They are **extrusive** because they **form on or near the surface**.

SEDIMENTARY ROCKS

Sedimentary rocks form from dead animal and plant remains (organic), small particles of land materials (clastic), and by physical changes in large bodies of water (precipitates and evaporites).

CLASTICS

Rain weathers and erodes the surface of the land. Materials that are eroded may eventually be deposited in the oceans.

After long periods and repeated burial, consolidation of rock particles occurs and sedimentary rocks are formed. Some examples of this are:

TYPE OF ROCK:	MADE UP OF:
Sandstone	particles of sand
Conglomerate	particles of gravel
Siltstone	fine particles of silt
Shale	particles of clay

ORGANIC

Organic rocks have their origin in living things.

TYPE OF ROCK:	MADE UP OF:
Coquina limestone	broken sea shells cemented together
Coal	decayed plant remains that are practically all carbon

CHEMICAL (EVAPORITES AND PRECIPITATES)

Occasionally, large bodies of the ocean become trapped on continents. In the past, trapped inland seas not only were denied an outlet to the ocean but did not have many contributing rivers. As a result, the sea water evaporated, leaving deposits of salts behind. A present-day example of this is the Great Salt Lake in Utah. This lake was once part of a larger lake called **Lake Bonneville,** which was once part of an inland sea.

Carbonates can, if sea H_2O is warmed sufficiently, precipitate and eventually form limestone.

METAMORPHIC ROCKS

Metamorphic means a change in form. Metamorphic rocks are sedimentary, igneous, or other metamorphic in origin. If the origin rocks are subjected to heat and pressure through burial or contact, rearrangement of particles or chemical composition occurs.

Some common examples of metamorphic changes in rocks are:

ORIGIN	METAMORPHIC
limestone	marble
shale	slate
sandstone	quartzite
any rock	gneiss or schists

THE ROCK CYCLE

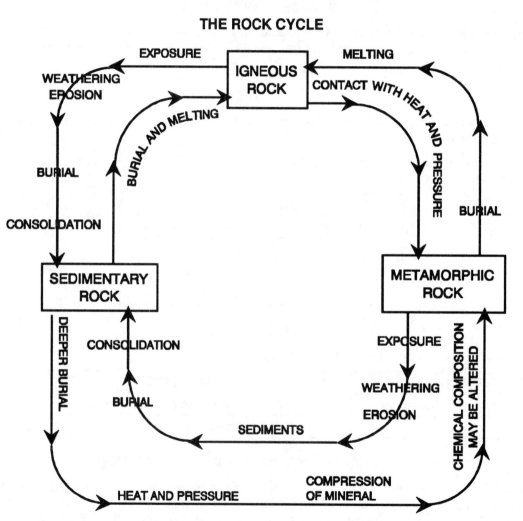

The rock cycle shows the path rocks may take depending upon the environment they are subjected to.

60

The Earth's History

After formation, a period of structuring the surface, atmosphere, and hydrosphere occurred. Sometime after the oceans and atmosphere evolved to what they basically are today, life began.

Our study of the earth's history is done by interpreting rocks and fossil remains. All the information can be gathered and placed into a "scale" based on years before present. This scale is called the Geologic Time Scale.

GEOLOGIC TIME SCALE

ERA	PERIOD	EPOCH	EVENTS OF IMPORTANCE	YEARS BEFORE PRESENT
CENOZOIC	QUATERNARY	RECENT PLEISTOCENE	MAN APPEARS ICE AGE	NOW 2 MIL. YEARS
CENOZOIC	TERTIARY	PLIOCENE MIOCENE OLIGOCENE EOCENE PALEOCENE	AGE OF MAMMALS	75 MIL. YEARS
MESOZOIC	CRETACEOUS JURASSIC TRIASSIC		AGE OF REPTILES PANGEA SUPERCONTINENT?	225 MIL. YEARS
PALEOZOIC	PERMIAN PENNSYLVANIAN MISSISSIPPIAN DEVONIAN SILURIAN ORDOVICIAN CAMBRIAN		AGE OF AMPHIBIANS COAL FORMING PERIOD AGE OF FISHES AGE OF INVERTEBRATES	350 MIL. YEARS 400 MIL. YEARS 600 MIL. YEARS
PROTEROZOIC			LIFE BEGINS IN THE OCEAN	3.3 BIL. YEARS
ARCHEOZOIC			NO LIFE	4.5 BIL. YEARS

HYDROSPHERE

The hydrosphere includes **all** the water on the surface of the earth. Most of this water is in the oceans. Approximately 70% of the earth's surface is covered with water.

As you know, sea water is salty. This is because water running over land dissolves salts and carries them to the sea.

One way of describing water is according to its **saline** content or salinity. Salinity is the amount of dissolved solids in water. In sea water, there are approximately 35 parts of dissolved solids per 1000 parts of sea water (3.5%).

Another characteristic of sea water is its temperature. The surface waters reflect the air temperature—in warm regions the water is relatively warm, and in cold regions the water is cold.

Differences in temperature cause differences in the density of sea water; and so the surface water circulates both horizontally and vertically. Bottom water in the oceans is close to 0°C (the freezing pt. of H_2O), but does not freeze because of the salinity and enormous pressures.

Ocean depths vary from 600 feet on the continental shelf to several miles for deep trenches. Generally, the sea floor is 2½-3 miles below the surface.

A profile of the ocean floor might look like this:

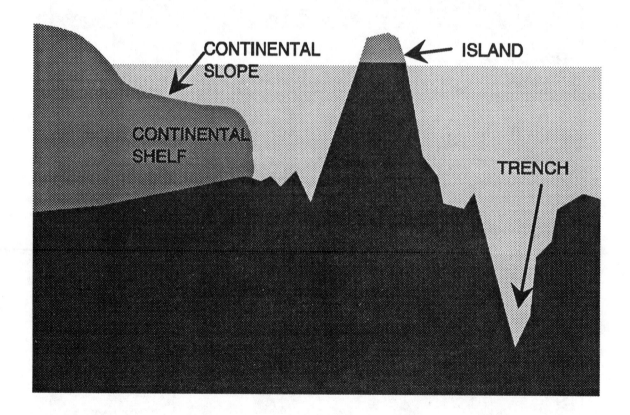

THE ATMOSPHERE

The atmosphere is composed of Oxygen (21%) and Nitrogen (78%). The other % is largely Argon, CO_2 and H_2O vapor. Most of the air is located close to the surface of the earth.

Physics Review

There are many areas that could be covered in this section of the book. However, many people who take the CLEP Examination have not studied physics formally. The presentation that follows is much like the chemistry section on the examination. This is information that you should know.

MOTION

Newton formulated the laws of motion in response to forces acting on a mass.

1ST LAW OF MOTION: A body at rest tends to stay at rest and a body in motion tends to stay in motion unless acted upon by some outside force.

2ND LAW OF MOTION: F = MA; Force is that quantity which causes a mass to accelerate.

3RD LAW OF MOTION: For every action there is an equal and opposite reaction.

To illustrate:

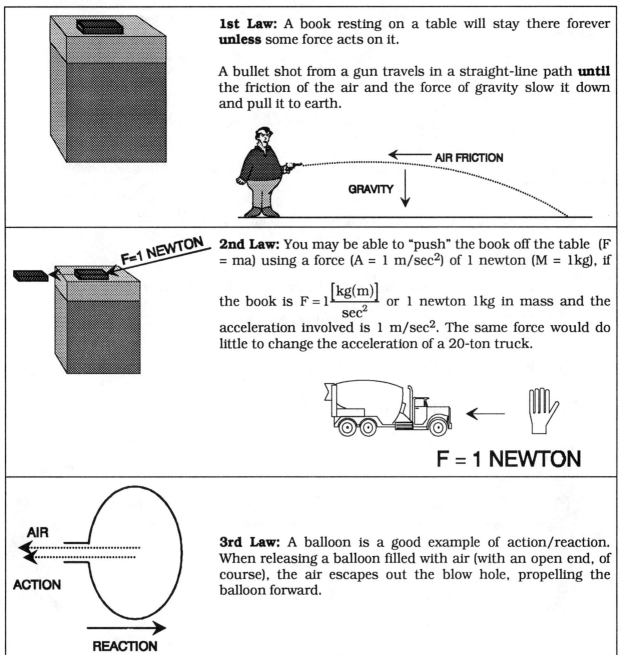

1st Law: A book resting on a table will stay there forever **unless** some force acts on it.

A bullet shot from a gun travels in a straight-line path **until** the friction of the air and the force of gravity slow it down and pull it to earth.

AIR FRICTION

GRAVITY

2nd Law: You may be able to "push" the book off the table (F = ma) using a force (A = 1 m/sec^2) of 1 newton (M = 1kg), if the book is $F = 1\dfrac{[\text{kg(m)}]}{\text{sec}^2}$ or 1 newton 1kg in mass and the acceleration involved is 1 m/sec^2. The same force would do little to change the acceleration of a 20-ton truck.

F=1 NEWTON

F = 1 NEWTON

AIR

ACTION

REACTION

3rd Law: A balloon is a good example of action/reaction. When releasing a balloon filled with air (with an open end, of course), the air escapes out the blow hole, propelling the balloon forward.

GRAVITY

GRAVITY

The formula involved is: $F = \dfrac{m_1 m_2}{d^2}$, where:

F = force of gravity

m_1 and m_2 = the masses of the bodies involved

d^2 = distance between the masses squared

The larger the masses, the greater the gravitational attraction between them (directly proportional).

EXAMPLE: Let $m_1 = 5$, $m_2 = 20$, and $d = 2$.   Then: $F = \dfrac{5 \times 20}{2^2} = \dfrac{100}{4} = 25$

Let m_1 increase to = 20.   Then: $F = \dfrac{20 \times 20}{2^2} = \dfrac{400}{4} = 100$

The larger the distances involved, the smaller the gravitational attraction between them (inversely proportional).

EXAMPLE: Let $m_1 = 5$, $m_2 = 20$, $d = 5$.   Then: $F = \dfrac{5 \times 20}{5^2} = \dfrac{100}{25} = 4$

Acceleration due to the force of gravity is:

$g = 32$ feet/sec^2 OR 980 cm/sec^2 OR 9.8 m/sec^2

EQUILIBRIUM

Equilibrium occurs when the sum of the forces acting on a body equals zero.

EXAMPLE: Each girl is pulling the rope exerting a 100 lb. pull:

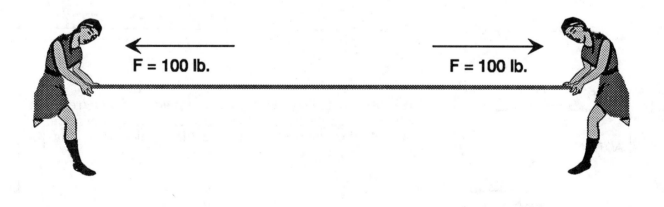

F = 100 lb.   F = 100 lb.

BOYLE'S LAW

Volume of a gas varies inversely with its pressure: $P \propto \dfrac{1}{V}$ if temperature remains constant.

As pressure increases, volume decreases.

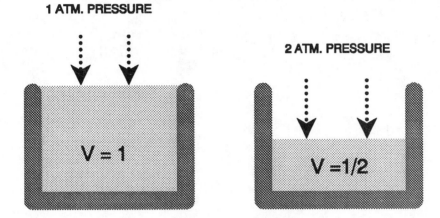

CHARLES' LAW

The volume of a gas is directly proportional to its temperature (when the pressure remains constant).

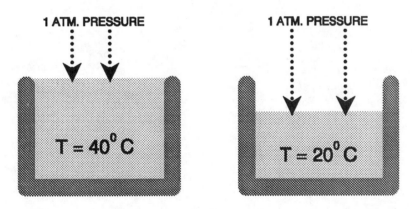

If the temperature (T) rises from 20°C to 40°C, the volume will also increase.

WORK

Any machine (lever, pulley, plane) may simplify work. By increasing the distance the force must act through, the input force number necessarily becomes smaller:

Work = force × distance

A screw is an example of an spiraling inclined plane.

Practice

The following pages provide you with answer sheets, a review test and answers, a glossary, tips on taking the CLEP examination, and a sample examination.

Answer Sheets

The following pages are copies* of the actual answer sheet you will use when you take a CLEP examination. The information requested must be filled in so that it can be read by a person and also by a computer. This means on page 1 and 2 of the answer sheet you will blacken the circle which has the same letter or number that appears at the top of that column. When you work in the test section, you will blacken the number you have chosen as the correct answer to the question.

With item Number 8, if you do not know the code number of the institution where you wish to have your scores sent, put four 9's in the spaces provided and indicate the name and address of the school. Enter four 0's if you wish to have your scores sent only to yourself.

It is important for you to understand the answer sheet **before** you go to take the test! Use it when you take your sample test.

SOME TIPS TO REMEMBER WHEN USING A SEPARATE ANSWER SHEET

1. Be **sure** you blacken the entire circle provided for your answer.

2. Be **sure** to put your answers at the proper place on the answer sheet. If you are answering question 30, be **sure** you record your answer at number 30 on the answer sheet.

3. Do **not** put any extra marks on your answer sheet. It may cause the question to be marked incorrect.

4. Be **sure** you record only **one** answer for each question. If you wish to change an answer, be **sure** you erase your first answer completely.

5. Use #2 lead pencils for the multiple choice answers.

*Reprinted and used with permission from <u>CLEP General and Subject Examinations</u>, copyright © 1986 by College Entrance Examination Board, New York.

COLLEGE-LEVEL EXAMINATION PROGRAM of the College Board
ANSWER SHEET FOR NATIONAL ADMINISTRATIONS — PAGE 1

Use only a soft lead (No. 2) pencil. Be sure each mark is dark and completely fills the intended oval. Erase any errors and stray marks completely.

1. YOUR NAME
Last Name — first 12 letters
First Name — first 8 letters
M.I.
Omit spaces, hyphens, apostrophes, and Jr. or II.

2. DATE OF BIRTH
Month	Day	Year
① Jan.		
② Feb.		
③ Mar.		
④ Apr.		
⑤ May		
⑥ Jun.		
⑦ Jul.		
⑧ Aug.		
⑨ Sep.		
⑩ Oct.		
⑪ Nov.		
⑫ Dec.		

3. SEX
Male ①
Female ②

4. SOCIAL SECURITY NUMBER
(Optional)

5. CURRENT EDUCATIONAL LEVEL
① High School
② High School Graduate
③ College Freshman
④ College Sophomore
⑤ College Junior
⑥ College Senior
⑦ College Graduate

6. ETHNIC GROUP
(Optional)
How do you describe yourself?
① American Indian, Eskimo or Aleut
② Black, Afro-American or Negro
③ Mexican American or Chicano
④ Oriental or Asian-American
⑤ Puerto Rican-American
⑥ Other Hispanic or Latin American
⑦ White or Caucasian
⑧ Other

7. TEST CENTER CODE NUMBER
Enter the code number in these boxes.

8. SCORE REPORT RECIPIENT
*Enter the Institution Code Number
Blacken the corresponding oval below each box
Institution Name and Location (Print)
Institution Name
City
State
*If you do not have the code number for the institution you want to receive your reports, enter 9999.

9. FEES PAID
See Admission Form.
Examination Fee . . . . $
Special Administration Fee (Fee is $10.) . . . . $
Total Paid . . . $

10. TOTAL NUMBER OF EXAMINATIONS YOU ARE GOING TO TAKE AT THIS ADMINISTRATION.
Blacken the corresponding oval below each box. →
○ 1   ○ 4   ○ 7   ○ 10
○ 2   ○ 5   ○ 8   ○ more than 10
○ 3   ○ 6   ○ 9

11. SIGNATURE AND DATE
I accept the conditions set forth in the Registration Guide concerning the administration of the tests and reporting of scores.
Today's Date:

DO NOT WRITE IN THIS BOX, FOR ETS USE ONLY.

DO NOT BACK FOLD THIS ANSWER SHEET.

I.N. 202853-185VV127P100

12. YOUR MAILING ADDRESS

Number and Street | City

A B C D E F G H I J K L M N O P Q R S T U V W X Y Z

0 1 2 3 4 5 6 7 8 9 /

ABBREVIATIONS FOR USE IN STREET ADDRESS

Avenue	AVE	Heights	HTS	Route	RTE
Boulevard	BLVD	Highway	HWY	Second	2ND
Circle	CIR	Mount	MT	South	S
Court	CT	North	N	Southeast	S E
Drive	DR	Northeast	N E	Southwest	S W
East	E	Northwest	N W	Square	SQ
Expressway	EXPWY	Parkway	PKY	Street	ST
First	1ST	Place	PL	Terrace	TER
Fort	FT	Post Office	P O	Third	3RD
Fourth	4TH	Road	RD	West	W

State

01	Alabama	12	Hawaii	23	Michigan	34	North Carolina	45	Utah
02	Alaska	13	Idaho	24	Minnesota	35	North Dakota	46	Vermont
03	Arizona	14	Illinois	25	Mississippi	36	Ohio	47	Virginia
04	Arkansas	15	Indiana	26	Missouri	37	Oklahoma	48	Washington
05	California	16	Iowa	27	Montana	38	Oregon	49	West Virginia
06	Colorado	17	Kansas	28	Nebraska	39	Pennsylvania	50	Wisconsin
07	Connecticut	18	Kentucky	29	Nevada	40	Rhode Island	51	Wyoming
08	Delaware	19	Louisiana	30	New Hampshire	41	South Carolina	52	Puerto Rico
09	Dist. of Col.	20	Maine	31	New Jersey	42	South Dakota	53	Foreign
10	Florida	21	Maryland	32	New Mexico	43	Tennessee		
11	Georgia	22	Massachusetts	33	New York	44	Texas		

U.S. Zip Code

0 1 2 3 4 5 6 7 8 9

Foreign Country Code

0 1 2 3 4 5 6 7 8 9

EXAMINATION #1

Your Name (Print): _____
　　　　　　　　　　　　　　Last　　　　　　　　First　　　　　　　M.I.

A. Print

Examination Name: _____ Form Designation: _____

B. TEST CODE	C. Are you going to take the optional essay portion of this examination?	D. TEST BOOK SERIAL NUMBER

C. Are you going to take the optional essay portion of this examination?

◯ 1　Yes

◯ 2　No

Be sure each mark is dark and completely fills the intended oval. If you erase, do so completely. You may find more answer responses than you need for one complete 90-minute examination. If so, please leave the extra ovals blank.

1 Ⓐ Ⓑ Ⓒ Ⓓ Ⓔ 31 Ⓐ Ⓑ Ⓒ Ⓓ Ⓔ 61 Ⓐ Ⓑ Ⓒ Ⓓ Ⓔ 91 Ⓐ Ⓑ Ⓒ Ⓓ Ⓔ 121 Ⓐ Ⓑ Ⓒ Ⓓ Ⓔ
2 Ⓐ Ⓑ Ⓒ Ⓓ Ⓔ 32 Ⓐ Ⓑ Ⓒ Ⓓ Ⓔ 62 Ⓐ Ⓑ Ⓒ Ⓓ Ⓔ 92 Ⓐ Ⓑ Ⓒ Ⓓ Ⓔ 122 Ⓐ Ⓑ Ⓒ Ⓓ Ⓔ
3 Ⓐ Ⓑ Ⓒ Ⓓ Ⓔ 33 Ⓐ Ⓑ Ⓒ Ⓓ Ⓔ 63 Ⓐ Ⓑ Ⓒ Ⓓ Ⓔ 93 Ⓐ Ⓑ Ⓒ Ⓓ Ⓔ 123 Ⓐ Ⓑ Ⓒ Ⓓ Ⓔ
4 Ⓐ Ⓑ Ⓒ Ⓓ Ⓔ 34 Ⓐ Ⓑ Ⓒ Ⓓ Ⓔ 64 Ⓐ Ⓑ Ⓒ Ⓓ Ⓔ 94 Ⓐ Ⓑ Ⓒ Ⓓ Ⓔ 124 Ⓐ Ⓑ Ⓒ Ⓓ Ⓔ
5 Ⓐ Ⓑ Ⓒ Ⓓ Ⓔ 35 Ⓐ Ⓑ Ⓒ Ⓓ Ⓔ 65 Ⓐ Ⓑ Ⓒ Ⓓ Ⓔ 95 Ⓐ Ⓑ Ⓒ Ⓓ Ⓔ 125 Ⓐ Ⓑ Ⓒ Ⓓ Ⓔ
6 Ⓐ Ⓑ Ⓒ Ⓓ Ⓔ 36 Ⓐ Ⓑ Ⓒ Ⓓ Ⓔ 66 Ⓐ Ⓑ Ⓒ Ⓓ Ⓔ 96 Ⓐ Ⓑ Ⓒ Ⓓ Ⓔ 126 Ⓐ Ⓑ Ⓒ Ⓓ Ⓔ
7 Ⓐ Ⓑ Ⓒ Ⓓ Ⓔ 37 Ⓐ Ⓑ Ⓒ Ⓓ Ⓔ 67 Ⓐ Ⓑ Ⓒ Ⓓ Ⓔ 97 Ⓐ Ⓑ Ⓒ Ⓓ Ⓔ 127 Ⓐ Ⓑ Ⓒ Ⓓ Ⓔ
8 Ⓐ Ⓑ Ⓒ Ⓓ Ⓔ 38 Ⓐ Ⓑ Ⓒ Ⓓ Ⓔ 68 Ⓐ Ⓑ Ⓒ Ⓓ Ⓔ 98 Ⓐ Ⓑ Ⓒ Ⓓ Ⓔ 128 Ⓐ Ⓑ Ⓒ Ⓓ Ⓔ
9 Ⓐ Ⓑ Ⓒ Ⓓ Ⓔ 39 Ⓐ Ⓑ Ⓒ Ⓓ Ⓔ 69 Ⓐ Ⓑ Ⓒ Ⓓ Ⓔ 99 Ⓐ Ⓑ Ⓒ Ⓓ Ⓔ 129 Ⓐ Ⓑ Ⓒ Ⓓ Ⓔ
10 Ⓐ Ⓑ Ⓒ Ⓓ Ⓔ 40 Ⓐ Ⓑ Ⓒ Ⓓ Ⓔ 70 Ⓐ Ⓑ Ⓒ Ⓓ Ⓔ 100 Ⓐ Ⓑ Ⓒ Ⓓ Ⓔ 130 Ⓐ Ⓑ Ⓒ Ⓓ Ⓔ
11 Ⓐ Ⓑ Ⓒ Ⓓ Ⓔ 41 Ⓐ Ⓑ Ⓒ Ⓓ Ⓔ 71 Ⓐ Ⓑ Ⓒ Ⓓ Ⓔ 101 Ⓐ Ⓑ Ⓒ Ⓓ Ⓔ 131 Ⓐ Ⓑ Ⓒ Ⓓ Ⓔ
12 Ⓐ Ⓑ Ⓒ Ⓓ Ⓔ 42 Ⓐ Ⓑ Ⓒ Ⓓ Ⓔ 72 Ⓐ Ⓑ Ⓒ Ⓓ Ⓔ 102 Ⓐ Ⓑ Ⓒ Ⓓ Ⓔ 132 Ⓐ Ⓑ Ⓒ Ⓓ Ⓔ
13 Ⓐ Ⓑ Ⓒ Ⓓ Ⓔ 43 Ⓐ Ⓑ Ⓒ Ⓓ Ⓔ 73 Ⓐ Ⓑ Ⓒ Ⓓ Ⓔ 103 Ⓐ Ⓑ Ⓒ Ⓓ Ⓔ 133 Ⓐ Ⓑ Ⓒ Ⓓ Ⓔ
14 Ⓐ Ⓑ Ⓒ Ⓓ Ⓔ 44 Ⓐ Ⓑ Ⓒ Ⓓ Ⓔ 74 Ⓐ Ⓑ Ⓒ Ⓓ Ⓔ 104 Ⓐ Ⓑ Ⓒ Ⓓ Ⓔ 134 Ⓐ Ⓑ Ⓒ Ⓓ Ⓔ
15 Ⓐ Ⓑ Ⓒ Ⓓ Ⓔ 45 Ⓐ Ⓑ Ⓒ Ⓓ Ⓔ 75 Ⓐ Ⓑ Ⓒ Ⓓ Ⓔ 105 Ⓐ Ⓑ Ⓒ Ⓓ Ⓔ 135 Ⓐ Ⓑ Ⓒ Ⓓ Ⓔ
16 Ⓐ Ⓑ Ⓒ Ⓓ Ⓔ 46 Ⓐ Ⓑ Ⓒ Ⓓ Ⓔ 76 Ⓐ Ⓑ Ⓒ Ⓓ Ⓔ 106 Ⓐ Ⓑ Ⓒ Ⓓ Ⓔ 136 Ⓐ Ⓑ Ⓒ Ⓓ Ⓔ
17 Ⓐ Ⓑ Ⓒ Ⓓ Ⓔ 47 Ⓐ Ⓑ Ⓒ Ⓓ Ⓔ 77 Ⓐ Ⓑ Ⓒ Ⓓ Ⓔ 107 Ⓐ Ⓑ Ⓒ Ⓓ Ⓔ 137 Ⓐ Ⓑ Ⓒ Ⓓ Ⓔ
18 Ⓐ Ⓑ Ⓒ Ⓓ Ⓔ 48 Ⓐ Ⓑ Ⓒ Ⓓ Ⓔ 78 Ⓐ Ⓑ Ⓒ Ⓓ Ⓔ 108 Ⓐ Ⓑ Ⓒ Ⓓ Ⓔ 138 Ⓐ Ⓑ Ⓒ Ⓓ Ⓔ
19 Ⓐ Ⓑ Ⓒ Ⓓ Ⓔ 49 Ⓐ Ⓑ Ⓒ Ⓓ Ⓔ 79 Ⓐ Ⓑ Ⓒ Ⓓ Ⓔ 109 Ⓐ Ⓑ Ⓒ Ⓓ Ⓔ 139 Ⓐ Ⓑ Ⓒ Ⓓ Ⓔ
20 Ⓐ Ⓑ Ⓒ Ⓓ Ⓔ 50 Ⓐ Ⓑ Ⓒ Ⓓ Ⓔ 80 Ⓐ Ⓑ Ⓒ Ⓓ Ⓔ 110 Ⓐ Ⓑ Ⓒ Ⓓ Ⓔ 140 Ⓐ Ⓑ Ⓒ Ⓓ Ⓔ
21 Ⓐ Ⓑ Ⓒ Ⓓ Ⓔ 51 Ⓐ Ⓑ Ⓒ Ⓓ Ⓔ 81 Ⓐ Ⓑ Ⓒ Ⓓ Ⓔ 111 Ⓐ Ⓑ Ⓒ Ⓓ Ⓔ 141 Ⓐ Ⓑ Ⓒ Ⓓ Ⓔ
22 Ⓐ Ⓑ Ⓒ Ⓓ Ⓔ 52 Ⓐ Ⓑ Ⓒ Ⓓ Ⓔ 82 Ⓐ Ⓑ Ⓒ Ⓓ Ⓔ 112 Ⓐ Ⓑ Ⓒ Ⓓ Ⓔ 142 Ⓐ Ⓑ Ⓒ Ⓓ Ⓔ
23 Ⓐ Ⓑ Ⓒ Ⓓ Ⓔ 53 Ⓐ Ⓑ Ⓒ Ⓓ Ⓔ 83 Ⓐ Ⓑ Ⓒ Ⓓ Ⓔ 113 Ⓐ Ⓑ Ⓒ Ⓓ Ⓔ 143 Ⓐ Ⓑ Ⓒ Ⓓ Ⓔ
24 Ⓐ Ⓑ Ⓒ Ⓓ Ⓔ 54 Ⓐ Ⓑ Ⓒ Ⓓ Ⓔ 84 Ⓐ Ⓑ Ⓒ Ⓓ Ⓔ 114 Ⓐ Ⓑ Ⓒ Ⓓ Ⓔ 144 Ⓐ Ⓑ Ⓒ Ⓓ Ⓔ
25 Ⓐ Ⓑ Ⓒ Ⓓ Ⓔ 55 Ⓐ Ⓑ Ⓒ Ⓓ Ⓔ 85 Ⓐ Ⓑ Ⓒ Ⓓ Ⓔ 115 Ⓐ Ⓑ Ⓒ Ⓓ Ⓔ 145 Ⓐ Ⓑ Ⓒ Ⓓ Ⓔ
26 Ⓐ Ⓑ Ⓒ Ⓓ Ⓔ 56 Ⓐ Ⓑ Ⓒ Ⓓ Ⓔ 86 Ⓐ Ⓑ Ⓒ Ⓓ Ⓔ 116 Ⓐ Ⓑ Ⓒ Ⓓ Ⓔ 146 Ⓐ Ⓑ Ⓒ Ⓓ Ⓔ
27 Ⓐ Ⓑ Ⓒ Ⓓ Ⓔ 57 Ⓐ Ⓑ Ⓒ Ⓓ Ⓔ 87 Ⓐ Ⓑ Ⓒ Ⓓ Ⓔ 117 Ⓐ Ⓑ Ⓒ Ⓓ Ⓔ 147 Ⓐ Ⓑ Ⓒ Ⓓ Ⓔ
28 Ⓐ Ⓑ Ⓒ Ⓓ Ⓔ 58 Ⓐ Ⓑ Ⓒ Ⓓ Ⓔ 88 Ⓐ Ⓑ Ⓒ Ⓓ Ⓔ 118 Ⓐ Ⓑ Ⓒ Ⓓ Ⓔ 148 Ⓐ Ⓑ Ⓒ Ⓓ Ⓔ
29 Ⓐ Ⓑ Ⓒ Ⓓ Ⓔ 59 Ⓐ Ⓑ Ⓒ Ⓓ Ⓔ 89 Ⓐ Ⓑ Ⓒ Ⓓ Ⓔ 119 Ⓐ Ⓑ Ⓒ Ⓓ Ⓔ 149 Ⓐ Ⓑ Ⓒ Ⓓ Ⓔ
30 Ⓐ Ⓑ Ⓒ Ⓓ Ⓔ 60 Ⓐ Ⓑ Ⓒ Ⓓ Ⓔ 90 Ⓐ Ⓑ Ⓒ Ⓓ Ⓔ 120 Ⓐ Ⓑ Ⓒ Ⓓ Ⓔ 150 Ⓐ Ⓑ Ⓒ Ⓓ Ⓔ

DO NOT WRITE IN THESE BOXES.

1R	1W	10	2R	2W	20	3R	3W	30	4R	4W	40	5R	5W	50	6R	6W	60	7R	7W	70	8R	8W	80

9R	9W	90	10R	10W	100	11R	11W	110	12R	12W	120	13R	13W	130	14R	14W	140	15R	15W	150	16R	16W	160

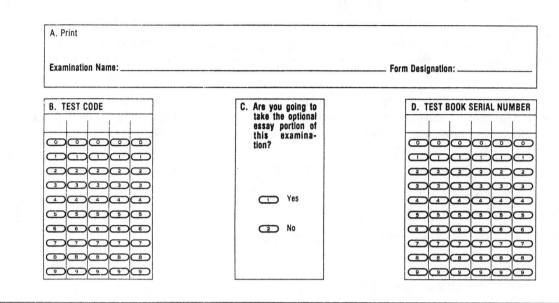

A. Print

Examination Name: _____ Form Designation: _____

B. TEST CODE

C. Are you going to take the optional essay portion of this examination?

- ⊂1⊃ Yes
- ⊂2⊃ No

D. TEST BOOK SERIAL NUMBER

Be sure each mark is dark and completely fills the intended oval. If you erase, do so completely. You may find more answer responses than you need for one complete 90-minute examination. If so, please leave the extra ovals blank.

1 Ⓐ Ⓑ Ⓒ Ⓓ Ⓔ	31 Ⓐ Ⓑ Ⓒ Ⓓ Ⓔ	61 Ⓐ Ⓑ Ⓒ Ⓓ Ⓔ	91 Ⓐ Ⓑ Ⓒ Ⓓ Ⓔ	121 Ⓐ Ⓑ Ⓒ Ⓓ Ⓔ
2 Ⓐ Ⓑ Ⓒ Ⓓ Ⓔ	32 Ⓐ Ⓑ Ⓒ Ⓓ Ⓔ	62 Ⓐ Ⓑ Ⓒ Ⓓ Ⓔ	92 Ⓐ Ⓑ Ⓒ Ⓓ Ⓔ	122 Ⓐ Ⓑ Ⓒ Ⓓ Ⓔ
3 Ⓐ Ⓑ Ⓒ Ⓓ Ⓔ	33 Ⓐ Ⓑ Ⓒ Ⓓ Ⓔ	63 Ⓐ Ⓑ Ⓒ Ⓓ Ⓔ	93 Ⓐ Ⓑ Ⓒ Ⓓ Ⓔ	123 Ⓐ Ⓑ Ⓒ Ⓓ Ⓔ
4 Ⓐ Ⓑ Ⓒ Ⓓ Ⓔ	34 Ⓐ Ⓑ Ⓒ Ⓓ Ⓔ	64 Ⓐ Ⓑ Ⓒ Ⓓ Ⓔ	94 Ⓐ Ⓑ Ⓒ Ⓓ Ⓔ	124 Ⓐ Ⓑ Ⓒ Ⓓ Ⓔ
5 Ⓐ Ⓑ Ⓒ Ⓓ Ⓔ	35 Ⓐ Ⓑ Ⓒ Ⓓ Ⓔ	65 Ⓐ Ⓑ Ⓒ Ⓓ Ⓔ	95 Ⓐ Ⓑ Ⓒ Ⓓ Ⓔ	125 Ⓐ Ⓑ Ⓒ Ⓓ Ⓔ
6 Ⓐ Ⓑ Ⓒ Ⓓ Ⓔ	36 Ⓐ Ⓑ Ⓒ Ⓓ Ⓔ	66 Ⓐ Ⓑ Ⓒ Ⓓ Ⓔ	96 Ⓐ Ⓑ Ⓒ Ⓓ Ⓔ	126 Ⓐ Ⓑ Ⓒ Ⓓ Ⓔ
7 Ⓐ Ⓑ Ⓒ Ⓓ Ⓔ	37 Ⓐ Ⓑ Ⓒ Ⓓ Ⓔ	67 Ⓐ Ⓑ Ⓒ Ⓓ Ⓔ	97 Ⓐ Ⓑ Ⓒ Ⓓ Ⓔ	127 Ⓐ Ⓑ Ⓒ Ⓓ Ⓔ
8 Ⓐ Ⓑ Ⓒ Ⓓ Ⓔ	38 Ⓐ Ⓑ Ⓒ Ⓓ Ⓔ	68 Ⓐ Ⓑ Ⓒ Ⓓ Ⓔ	98 Ⓐ Ⓑ Ⓒ Ⓓ Ⓔ	128 Ⓐ Ⓑ Ⓒ Ⓓ Ⓔ
9 Ⓐ Ⓑ Ⓒ Ⓓ Ⓔ	39 Ⓐ Ⓑ Ⓒ Ⓓ Ⓔ	69 Ⓐ Ⓑ Ⓒ Ⓓ Ⓔ	99 Ⓐ Ⓑ Ⓒ Ⓓ Ⓔ	129 Ⓐ Ⓑ Ⓒ Ⓓ Ⓔ
10 Ⓐ Ⓑ Ⓒ Ⓓ Ⓔ	40 Ⓐ Ⓑ Ⓒ Ⓓ Ⓔ	70 Ⓐ Ⓑ Ⓒ Ⓓ Ⓔ	100 Ⓐ Ⓑ Ⓒ Ⓓ Ⓔ	130 Ⓐ Ⓑ Ⓒ Ⓓ Ⓔ
11 Ⓐ Ⓑ Ⓒ Ⓓ Ⓔ	41 Ⓐ Ⓑ Ⓒ Ⓓ Ⓔ	71 Ⓐ Ⓑ Ⓒ Ⓓ Ⓔ	101 Ⓐ Ⓑ Ⓒ Ⓓ Ⓔ	131 Ⓐ Ⓑ Ⓒ Ⓓ Ⓔ
12 Ⓐ Ⓑ Ⓒ Ⓓ Ⓔ	42 Ⓐ Ⓑ Ⓒ Ⓓ Ⓔ	72 Ⓐ Ⓑ Ⓒ Ⓓ Ⓔ	102 Ⓐ Ⓑ Ⓒ Ⓓ Ⓔ	132 Ⓐ Ⓑ Ⓒ Ⓓ Ⓔ
13 Ⓐ Ⓑ Ⓒ Ⓓ Ⓔ	43 Ⓐ Ⓑ Ⓒ Ⓓ Ⓔ	73 Ⓐ Ⓑ Ⓒ Ⓓ Ⓔ	103 Ⓐ Ⓑ Ⓒ Ⓓ Ⓔ	133 Ⓐ Ⓑ Ⓒ Ⓓ Ⓔ
14 Ⓐ Ⓑ Ⓒ Ⓓ Ⓔ	44 Ⓐ Ⓑ Ⓒ Ⓓ Ⓔ	74 Ⓐ Ⓑ Ⓒ Ⓓ Ⓔ	104 Ⓐ Ⓑ Ⓒ Ⓓ Ⓔ	134 Ⓐ Ⓑ Ⓒ Ⓓ Ⓔ
15 Ⓐ Ⓑ Ⓒ Ⓓ Ⓔ	45 Ⓐ Ⓑ Ⓒ Ⓓ Ⓔ	75 Ⓐ Ⓑ Ⓒ Ⓓ Ⓔ	105 Ⓐ Ⓑ Ⓒ Ⓓ Ⓔ	135 Ⓐ Ⓑ Ⓒ Ⓓ Ⓔ
16 Ⓐ Ⓑ Ⓒ Ⓓ Ⓔ	46 Ⓐ Ⓑ Ⓒ Ⓓ Ⓔ	76 Ⓐ Ⓑ Ⓒ Ⓓ Ⓔ	106 Ⓐ Ⓑ Ⓒ Ⓓ Ⓔ	136 Ⓐ Ⓑ Ⓒ Ⓓ Ⓔ
17 Ⓐ Ⓑ Ⓒ Ⓓ Ⓔ	47 Ⓐ Ⓑ Ⓒ Ⓓ Ⓔ	77 Ⓐ Ⓑ Ⓒ Ⓓ Ⓔ	107 Ⓐ Ⓑ Ⓒ Ⓓ Ⓔ	137 Ⓐ Ⓑ Ⓒ Ⓓ Ⓔ
18 Ⓐ Ⓑ Ⓒ Ⓓ Ⓔ	48 Ⓐ Ⓑ Ⓒ Ⓓ Ⓔ	78 Ⓐ Ⓑ Ⓒ Ⓓ Ⓔ	108 Ⓐ Ⓑ Ⓒ Ⓓ Ⓔ	138 Ⓐ Ⓑ Ⓒ Ⓓ Ⓔ
19 Ⓐ Ⓑ Ⓒ Ⓓ Ⓔ	49 Ⓐ Ⓑ Ⓒ Ⓓ Ⓔ	79 Ⓐ Ⓑ Ⓒ Ⓓ Ⓔ	109 Ⓐ Ⓑ Ⓒ Ⓓ Ⓔ	139 Ⓐ Ⓑ Ⓒ Ⓓ Ⓔ
20 Ⓐ Ⓑ Ⓒ Ⓓ Ⓔ	50 Ⓐ Ⓑ Ⓒ Ⓓ Ⓔ	80 Ⓐ Ⓑ Ⓒ Ⓓ Ⓔ	110 Ⓐ Ⓑ Ⓒ Ⓓ Ⓔ	140 Ⓐ Ⓑ Ⓒ Ⓓ Ⓔ
21 Ⓐ Ⓑ Ⓒ Ⓓ Ⓔ	51 Ⓐ Ⓑ Ⓒ Ⓓ Ⓔ	81 Ⓐ Ⓑ Ⓒ Ⓓ Ⓔ	111 Ⓐ Ⓑ Ⓒ Ⓓ Ⓔ	141 Ⓐ Ⓑ Ⓒ Ⓓ Ⓔ
22 Ⓐ Ⓑ Ⓒ Ⓓ Ⓔ	52 Ⓐ Ⓑ Ⓒ Ⓓ Ⓔ	82 Ⓐ Ⓑ Ⓒ Ⓓ Ⓔ	112 Ⓐ Ⓑ Ⓒ Ⓓ Ⓔ	142 Ⓐ Ⓑ Ⓒ Ⓓ Ⓔ
23 Ⓐ Ⓑ Ⓒ Ⓓ Ⓔ	53 Ⓐ Ⓑ Ⓒ Ⓓ Ⓔ	83 Ⓐ Ⓑ Ⓒ Ⓓ Ⓔ	113 Ⓐ Ⓑ Ⓒ Ⓓ Ⓔ	143 Ⓐ Ⓑ Ⓒ Ⓓ Ⓔ
24 Ⓐ Ⓑ Ⓒ Ⓓ Ⓔ	54 Ⓐ Ⓑ Ⓒ Ⓓ Ⓔ	84 Ⓐ Ⓑ Ⓒ Ⓓ Ⓔ	114 Ⓐ Ⓑ Ⓒ Ⓓ Ⓔ	144 Ⓐ Ⓑ Ⓒ Ⓓ Ⓔ
25 Ⓐ Ⓑ Ⓒ Ⓓ Ⓔ	55 Ⓐ Ⓑ Ⓒ Ⓓ Ⓔ	85 Ⓐ Ⓑ Ⓒ Ⓓ Ⓔ	115 Ⓐ Ⓑ Ⓒ Ⓓ Ⓔ	145 Ⓐ Ⓑ Ⓒ Ⓓ Ⓔ
26 Ⓐ Ⓑ Ⓒ Ⓓ Ⓔ	56 Ⓐ Ⓑ Ⓒ Ⓓ Ⓔ	86 Ⓐ Ⓑ Ⓒ Ⓓ Ⓔ	116 Ⓐ Ⓑ Ⓒ Ⓓ Ⓔ	146 Ⓐ Ⓑ Ⓒ Ⓓ Ⓔ
27 Ⓐ Ⓑ Ⓒ Ⓓ Ⓔ	57 Ⓐ Ⓑ Ⓒ Ⓓ Ⓔ	87 Ⓐ Ⓑ Ⓒ Ⓓ Ⓔ	117 Ⓐ Ⓑ Ⓒ Ⓓ Ⓔ	147 Ⓐ Ⓑ Ⓒ Ⓓ Ⓔ
28 Ⓐ Ⓑ Ⓒ Ⓓ Ⓔ	58 Ⓐ Ⓑ Ⓒ Ⓓ Ⓔ	88 Ⓐ Ⓑ Ⓒ Ⓓ Ⓔ	118 Ⓐ Ⓑ Ⓒ Ⓓ Ⓔ	148 Ⓐ Ⓑ Ⓒ Ⓓ Ⓔ
29 Ⓐ Ⓑ Ⓒ Ⓓ Ⓔ	59 Ⓐ Ⓑ Ⓒ Ⓓ Ⓔ	89 Ⓐ Ⓑ Ⓒ Ⓓ Ⓔ	119 Ⓐ Ⓑ Ⓒ Ⓓ Ⓔ	149 Ⓐ Ⓑ Ⓒ Ⓓ Ⓔ
30 Ⓐ Ⓑ Ⓒ Ⓓ Ⓔ	60 Ⓐ Ⓑ Ⓒ Ⓓ Ⓔ	90 Ⓐ Ⓑ Ⓒ Ⓓ Ⓔ	120 Ⓐ Ⓑ Ⓒ Ⓓ Ⓔ	150 Ⓐ Ⓑ Ⓒ Ⓓ Ⓔ

DO NOT WRITE IN THESE BOXES.

1R	1W	10	2R	2W	20	3R	3W	30	4R	4W	40	5R	5W	50	6R	6W	60	7R	7W	70	8R	8W	80

9R	9W	90	10R	10W	100	11R	11W	110	12R	12W	120	13R	13W	130	14R	14W	140	15R	15W	150	16R	16W	160

Review Test

Questions in the following review test are taken from the material presented in this text. After reading the text, you should be able to answer a high percentage of the forty-four questions asked.

Unlike the sample tests in Biology and Physical Science which follow the glossary, no explanations are provided with the answer key. Rather, a page reference is provided so that you are directed to the page where the correct answer can be found for problems answered incorrectly.

Work slowly and carefully when you take this examination. It is not designed to be completed in a certain time period.

Practice the test-taking techniques which are important.

1.   Choose a quiet spot where you will not be disturbed.

2.   Use the coding system explained on page VI.

3.   Use the separate answer sheet provided.

Correct the test.

Review those pages indicated by your incorrect answers.

REVIEW TEST

1. The function of the circulatory system is

   (A) removal of wastes
   (B) exchange of gases
   (C) regulation of body temperature
   (D) protection
   (E) all of the above

2. White blood cells are called

   (A) leukocytes
   (B) platelets
   (C) erythrocytes
   (D) thrombocytes
   (E) plasma

3. The part of the heart that pumps blood out into the body is the

   (A) right atrium
   (B) right ventricule
   (C) left atrium
   (D) left ventricule
   (E) aorta

4. Heart rate is associated with

   (A) musculatory system
   (B) circulatory system
   (C) central nervous system
   (D) autonomic nervous system
   (E) endocrine system

5. The unique characteristic of starfish is their

   (A) ability to reproduce sexually
   (B) water vascular system
   (C) five rays
   (D) marine habitat
   (E) dependence on diatoms for nutrition

6. Plant cells differ from animal cells because they possess

   (A) vacuoles
   (B) cell walls
   (C) a nucleus
   (D) chromosomes
   (E) cell membranes

7. The stigma of a plant is part of the

   (A) support tissue which provides rigidity
   (B) cambium
   (C) reproductive system
   (D) xylem
   (E) circulatory system regulating water in the leaf

8. Messenger RNA are formed by

   (A) transfer RNA
   (B) enzymes
   (C) copying DNA in the nucleus
   (D) amino acids
   (E) viruses

9. This protist forms a geometric, silica shell and stores its food as oil

   (A) virus
   (B) bacilli
   (C) fungi
   (D) sponges
   (E) diatoms

10. The change from a three-chambered heart to a four-chambered heart occurs between

    (A) pisces and amphibians
    (B) amphibians and reptiles
    (C) reptiles and aves
    (D) aves and chordates
    (E) chordates and pisces

11. Spirogyra, a protist algae, may reproduce by the process of conjugation. The animal protist which has the ability to reproduce by the process of conjugation is

    (A) paramecium
    (B) streptococcus
    (C) lichen
    (D) slime mold
    (E) amoeba

12. Atoms are made of the following particles

    (A) neutrons, protons, nuclei
    (B) electrons, protons, orbits
    (C) protons, nuclei, electrons
    (D) electrons, protons, neutrons
    (E) nuclei, orbits, levels

13. The number of protons and electrons determine the atom's

    (A) atomic weight
    (B) chemical properties
    (C) physical properties
    (D) nuclear properties
    (E) chemical and physical properties

14. Which of the following elements exist as diatomic gases?

    (A) N, O Cl, H
    (B) K, Na, Cl, Mg
    (C) Br, Hg, K, H
    (D) N, C, O, H
    (E) H_2O, NaCl, K, O

15. Which of the following combinations may form compounds?

    (A) element + element
    (B) compound + compound
    (C) compound + element
    (D) element + compound + compound
    (E) all of the above

16. In order to satisfy the Law of Conservation of Matter, we adjust the number of _?_ to achieve a balance in the chemical equation.

    (A) molecules
    (B) electrons
    (C) protons
    (D) neutrons
    (E) nuclei

17. Sharing electrons is a characteristic of

    (A) ions
    (B) isotopes
    (C) isobars
    (D) covalent molecules
    (E) monoatomic atoms

18. The loss of a beta particle during radioactive decay results in

    (A) loss of atomic weight, gain in atomic number
    (B) gain in atomic weight, gain in atomic number
    (C) loss of atomic weight, loss in atomic number
    (D) no change of atomic weight, loss in atomic number
    (E) no change of atomic weight, gain in atomic number

19. $F = \dfrac{m_1 m_2}{d^2}$ is a formula used to calculate

    (A) intensity of light
    (B) the strength of magnetic energy
    (C) gravitational attraction
    (D) the speed of light
    (E) pressure

20. Acceleration due to the force of gravity is

   (A) 9.8 m/sec^2
   (B) 980 m/sec^2
   (C) 32 m/sec^2
   (D) $186,000 \text{ mi/sec}$
   (E) $6,000,000,000,000 \text{ mi/yr}$

21. Which of the following is most like an inclined plane?

   (A) crowbar
   (B) pulley
   (C) gear
   (D) scissors
   (E) screw

22. Which one of the following people is given credit for establishing Radio Astronomy as a branch of astronomy?

   (A) Galileo
   (B) Newton
   (C) Watson
   (D) Weiszacker
   (E) Jansky

23. Jupiter is flattened at its poles because of its

   (A) fast rotation
   (B) size
   (C) atmospheric composition
   (D) large number of satellites
   (E) Red Spot

24. Our galaxy is shaped like

   (A) a barred-spiral galaxy
   (B) an elliptical galaxy
   (C) a spiral galaxy
   (D) a two-armed spiral galaxy
   (E) the sun

25. A theory concerning the formation of the solar system is

   (A) Oscillating
   (B) Big Bang
   (C) Protoplanet
   (D) Steady-state
   (E) Atomic

26. The composition of the Sun is mainly

   (A) H_2
   (B) O_2
   (C) Fe
   (D) He
   (E) H_2O

27. The largest planet is

   (A) Mercury
   (B) Earth
   (C) Jupiter
   (D) Uranus
   (E) Pluto

28. The planet whose atmospheric composition is N_2 and O_2 is

   (A) Venus
   (B) Earth
   (C) Mars
   (D) Jupiter
   (E) Pluto

29. The age of the earth is

   (A) 4,500 years
   (B) 186,000 years
   (C) 6 trillion years
   (D) a light year
   (E) 4.5 billion years

30. The part of the earth that is thought to exist in a liquid-like state is

   (A) crust
   (B) mantle
   (C) outer core
   (D) inner core
   (E) basalt bedrock of the ocean floor

31. Secondary waves generated by earthquakes do not pass through the

   (A) crust
   (B) mantle
   (C) outer core
   (D) inner core
   (E) granite rock of the continents

32. A rift-valley may form as a result of

   (A) sea-floor spreading
   (B) volcanoes erupting
   (C) colliding plates on the surface of the earth
   (D) subduction
   (E) island formation

33. Mountains may be formed by

   (A) sea-floor spreading
   (B) colliding continental plates
   (C) subsiding sea-floor activity
   (D) erosion
   (E) rift valleys

34. Igneous rocks form from

   (A) sediments
   (B) weathering and erosion
   (C) intense pressure and heat
   (D) magma and lava
   (E) earthquakes

35. The metamorphic rock, marble, is formed from

   (A) basalt
   (B) sandstone
   (C) shale
   (D) granite
   (E) limestone

36. The correct order, from oldest to youngest is

   (A) life in the oceans, age of mammals, age of fishes
   (B) no life, age of invertebrates, age of amphibians
   (C) age of mammals, age of reptiles, age of amphibians
   (D) age of invertebrates, age of amphibians, age of fishes
   (E) age of reptiles, age of mammals, age of amphibians

37. "Weather" occurs in the

   (A) stratosphere
   (B) troposphere
   (C) mesosphere
   (D) thermosphere
   (E) exosphere

38. The average depth of the ocean floor is

   (A) 600 feet
   (B) 1 mile
   (C) 2 ½ - 3 miles
   (D) 5 miles
   (E) 7 miles

39. An insect that does NOT go through metamorphosis is

   (A) wasp
   (B) moth
   (C) fly
   (D) grasshopper
   (E) butterfly

40. The cross between two heterozygous black cows (Bb) produces

   (A) one pure black, two hybrid black, one pure white
   (B) three pure black, one pure white
   (C) four hybrid black
   (D) four pure white
   (E) one pure black, two hybrid white, one pure white

41. The distance of the earth from the sun is

    (A) 186,000 miles
    (B) 4.3 light years
    (C) 6 trillion miles
    (D) 93 million miles
    (E) 846,000 miles

42. Gregor Mendel is famous for his work with

    (A) Continental Drift Theory
    (B) laws of motion
    (C) Protoplanet hypothesis
    (D) molecular structure of DNA
    (E) laws of genetics

43. Which of the below is the most developed in terms of systems of the soft-bodies animals?

    (A) sponges
    (B) jellyfish
    (C) roundworms
    (D) flatworms
    (E) segmented worms

44. Parallel-veined leaves are typical of

    (A) maple trees
    (B) pine trees
    (C) mosses
    (D) ferns
    (E) grasses

REVIEW TEST ANSWERS

1.	(E)	p. 25		23.	(A)	p. 54
2.	(A)	p. 25		24.	(D)	p. 50
3.	(D)	p. 26		25.	(C)	p. 50
4.	(D)	p. 27		26.	(A)	p. 51
5.	(B)	p. 23		27.	(C)	p. 54
6.	(B)	p. 3		28.	(B)	p. 53
7.	(C)	p. 19		29.	(E)	p. 55
8.	(C)	p. 5		30.	(C)	p. 55
9.	(E)	p. 16		31.	(C)	p. 56
10.	(B)	p. 24		32.	(A)	p. 57
11.	(A)	p. 14		33.	(B)	p. 58
12.	(D)	p. 30		34.	(D)	p. 59
13.	(E)	p. 30		35.	(E)	p. 60
14.	(A)	p. 33		36.	(B)	p. 61
15.	(E)	p. 34		37.	(B)	p. 63
16.	(A)	p. 35		38.	(C)	p. 76
17.	(D)	p. 36		39.	(D)	p. 23
18.	(E)	p. 38		40.	(A)	p. 11, 12
19.	(C)	p. 65		41.	(D)	p. 53
20.	(A)	p. 65		42.	(E)	p. 11
21.	(E)	p. 67		43.	(E)	p. 21
22.	(E)	p. 47		44.	(E)	p. 18

Review those pages indicated by your incorrect answers.

Glossary

ABSOLUTE ZERO	The temperature at which matter has lost all its thermal energy. [0°K, - 273°C, - 459.7°F].
ACCRETION	The growing together of plant or animal tissues that are normally separate.
ACID	A substance in which H acts as a metal (+ ion).
ADP	Adenosine diphosphate, a compound involved with energy storage and release in the cell.
AEROBIC	Relating to a living organism that requires atmospheric oxygen.
AIR MASS	A body of air having common characteristics.
ALIMENTARY CANAL	The food tube in animals.
ALLELE	One of a pair of genes.
ALLOY	A material composed of two or more metals.
ALTIMETER	An instrument used to measure altitude.
AMMETER	An instrument used to measure the flow of electricity.
AMP	A unit of current equaling one coulomb per second.
ANAEROBIC	Relating to organisms unable to survive in atmospheric oxygen.
ANEMOMETER	An instrument that measures wind speed.
ANGSTROM	A linear measurement equal to 1×10^{-8} (0.00000001 cm).
ANHYDROUS	Without H_2O.
ANODE	Positive electrical terminal in an electric cell.
ANTIBIOTIC	A substance produced by molds, fungi, or bacteria. Used to cure bacterial infections.
AORTA	The large artery leaving the heart to the body.
APOGEE	The point at which an orbiting satellite is farthest from earth.
AQUIFER	A layer of rock that holds H_2O.
ARCHAEOPTERYX	The first bird.
ARTERY	Large blood vessels carrying oxygenated blood away from the heart.
ASEXUAL REPRODUCTION	Reproduction without sperm and eggs.
ASTRONOMICAL UNIT	Distance between the earth and sun—93,000,000 miles.
ATOMIC WEIGHT	The relative weight of an atom, compared to the standard $-C^{12}$.
ATP	Adenosine triphosphate, a compound involved with energy storage and release in the cell.
AXON	A part of the nerve cell that conducts electrical impulses away from the cell body.
BAROMETER	An instrument used to measure air pressure.

BASE	A substance which combines with hydroxyl ions.
BINARY STAR	Two stars revolving around each other.
BROWNIAN MOVEMENT	The erratic movement of particles due to collisions with atomic or molecular matter.
BTU	British Thermal Unit, a unit of heat energy needed to raise the temperature of one pound H_2O one degree F.
BUFFER	A substance which will resist any change in the pH of a solution.
CALORIE	A unit of heat energy needed to raise one gram of H_2O one degree C.
CATALYST	A substance that controls the rate of a chemical reaction.
CATHODE	Negative electrical terminal in an electric cell.
CENTRAL NERVOUS SYSTEM	Brain and spinal cord.
CENTRIFUGAL REACTION	The reaction of a body to centripetal force.
CENTRIPETAL FORCE	The force that causes a body to conform to movement around a curve.
CEREBELLUM	The part of the brain involved with balance and muscle coordination.
CEREBRUM	The part of the brain involved with intelligence.
CHLOROPHYLL	Green substance used in the food manufacturing process in plants.
CHRONOMETER	A ship's clock which is used to determine longitude.
COELOM	A space forming the body cavity of an animal.
COLLOID	A particle suspended in a medium (most often, liquid).
COLOR	That property of light related to wavelength.
CONDENSATION NUCLEI	The "seeds" upon which H_2O molecules will condense, forming cloud droplets.
CORIOLIS EFFECT	The deflection of the atmosphere and ocean currents due to the earth's rotation.
COTYLEDON	A thick food leaf formed from the seed of a newly germinated plant.
CROSS-POLLINATION	The movement of pollen from one plant to another plant.
CRYOGENICS	The science of low temperature phenomena.
CURIE	A unit of radioactivity.
DECIBEL	A unit of sound level intensity.
DECIDUOUS	Relating to woody plants that lose their leaves in winter.
DENDRITE	A part of the nerve that conducts electrical impulse to the cell body.

DENSITY	$D = \dfrac{m}{v}$, mass per unit volume.
DEW POINT	The temperature at which the air is saturated with H_2O vapor.
DIAPHRAGM	Muscular separation between the chest and abdominal cavities.
DICOTYLEDON	Two thick food leaves formed from the seed of a newly germinated plant.
DIFFUSION	The spreading out of particles to fill a space.
DNA	Deoxyribonucleic acid. A large molecule that controls cell functions. Contains cell's genetic information.
DOPPLER EFFECT	The apparent change in the wavelength of energy emitted by a source as determined by the receiver.
DORSAL	Relating to upper or "back" surface of an animal.
DYNE	A unit of force; 1 dyne = $\dfrac{1 \text{ gram}}{cm / sec^2}$.
ECOLOGY	The study of the relationship between organisms and their environment.
ECTODERM	Outer layer of cells in an animal body.
EFFERVESCENCE	The rapid escape of gas from a liquid (i.e. soda).
EFFICIENCY	The comparison of work input of a machine to its work output.
ENDODERM	Inner layer of cells in an animal body.
ENDOTHERMIC	The absorption of heat energy during a chemical reaction.
ENERGY LEVEL	The location around the nucleus where electrons are found.
ENZYME	Catalyst used in chemical reactions in cells (suffix is often "ase").
EPICENTER	Point on the surface of the earth that is directly above the focus of an earthquake.
EQUILIBRIUM	A situation in which two opposite processes occur at the same rate (water 32°F ice).
EQUINOX	The days when the sun's direct rays strike perpendicularly at the equator (March 21 and September 21).
ERG	Unit of work; 1 erg = 1 dyne × 1 cm.
EROSION	Movement of sediments by wind, water, and ice.
EUTROPHICATION	Aging of ponds or lakes as plants and sediments fill them in.
EVOLUTION	The gradual change of organisms with respect to acquired traits.
EXOTHERMIC	Relating to the release of heat energy during a chemical reaction.
EXTRUSIVE ROCKS	Igneous rocks that form on or near the surface.
FAULT	A break in rocks along which movement has occurred.
FERTILIZATION	The joining together of sperm and egg.
FIBRINOGEN	A protein present in blood which aids in clotting.

FIRN	Snow or ice pellets that become part of a glacier.
FISSION	The breakup of a heavy nucleus into two smaller weighted nuclei.
FOCUS	The point in the earth's crust where an earthquake originates.
FORCE	That action which produces or prevents changes in motion.
FOSSIL	Remains or evidence of life as it was in the past.
FOVEA	A part of the eye which has many cones.
FREQUENCY	Number of cycles per unit time.
FRICTION	A force that opposes motion.
FRONT	The line along which two air masses collide.
FRUIT	An ovary.
FULCRUM	A pivot point.
FUSION	The combining of two lightweight nuclei into one heavy nucleus.
GALVANIZE	To coat Fe or steel with Zn.
GAMETOPHYTE	A stage in reproduction in which gametes are formed.
GASTRULA	The early stage of development when germ layers appear.
GEIGER COUNTER	An instrument that detects radioactivity.
GENE	A portion of the DNA molecule that produces a trait in the organism.
GENETIC CODE	The chemical sequence in DNA that produces a trait.
GEOSYNCLINE	Downfold of the earth's crust which is being filled with sediments.
GEOTROPISM	Response of plants to gravity.
GEYSER	Steam and hot water that erupt from cracks in the earth's surface.
GILL	An organ used to remove O_2 from water H_2O.
GLACIER	A moving body of ice.
GLUCOSE	A simple sugar.
GONADS	Male and female reproductive organs.
HARD WATER	H_2O containing dissolved minerals.
HEAT OF FORMATION	The amount of heat needed or released when a compound is formed.
HERBACEOUS	Relating to the stem of a plant that lives only one season.
HERBIVORES	Plant-eating animals.
HEREDITY	The passing of traits from parents to offspring.
HORIZON	A line of vision where the surface meets the sky.
HORSEPOWER	A unit of power equal to 550 ft.-lb./sec.
HOST	An organism used by a parasite to supply it with food.

HUMUS	Decayed organic matter.
HYDRATION	The attachment of H_2O molecules to a particle of matter.
HYGROMETER	An instrument that determines relative humidity.
HYPOTHESIS	A possible explanation.
IGNEOUS ROCKS	Rocks that form from liquid rock (lava/magma).
INORGANIC	Materials which are *not* hydrocarbons.
INSOLATION	Incoming solar radiation.
INSULATOR	A poor conductor of heat or electricity.
INSULIN	A hormone produced by the pancreas to regulate the oxidation of sugar in cells.
INTERNATIONAL DATE-LINE	The 180° east or west longitude line (bent for convenience) that separates dates east and west (crossing over the dateline east to west—gain a day; west to east—lose a day).
INTRUSIVE ROCKS	Igneous rocks that form deep within the earth's crust.
INVERTEBRATE	Animal lacking a backbone.
IRIS	Colored portion of the eye.
ISO	Prefix meaning "the same."
ISOBAR	A line connecting points of equal air pressure on a weather map.
JOULE	Unit of work equaling 1 nt. × 1 m.
KINETIC ENERGY	Energy of motion.
KNOT	One nautical mile/hour.
LACTASE	An enzyme used to change lactose to glucose.
LATITUDE	Degrees north or south of the equator.
LAVA	Molten rock that reaches the earth's surface.
LEVER	A bar used as a simple machine.
LIGHT REACTION	First stage of photosynthesis in which energy is produced and used to split H_2O molecules.
LIPASE	An enzyme used to change fat into fatty acids and glycerin.
LITHOSPHERE	Crust of the earth.
LOCAL NOON	The time at which the sun in its transit across the sky crosses the observer's meridian (longitude).
LONGITUDE	Degrees east or west of the Prime Meridian.
LUNAR MONTH	29½ days.
LUNG	An organ used by air-breathing animals.
LUSTER	Shine of a mineral surface (metallic, earthy, pearly, glassy, etc.).
MAGMA	Liquid rock that is located deep within the earth's crust.
MAGNITUDE	The *apparent* brightness of a star.

MANOMETER	An instrument used to measure gas pressure.
MARE	Latin word meaning "sea."
MARROW	Soft interior part of bones.
MASS	The measure of the amount of matter that a body has.
MEDULLA OBLONGATA	Large part of the spinal cord next to the brain.
MEIOSIS	Sex cell formation. Reduction of chromosomes from a diploid number to a haploid number.
MERIDIAN	An imaginary line from pole to pole; longitude line.
MESODERM	Middle layer of cells in an animal body.
MESOZOIC ERA	Age of the reptiles.
MESSENGER RNA	M-RNA. RNA molecules that are fashioned from the DNA in the nucleus of the cell. Travel from nucleus to cytoplasm to the site where information will be transferred via "fashioning" to transfer RNA's.
METAL	Elements which readily donate electrons in chemical reactions; have luster, are good conductors, and are malleable.
METAMORPHIC ROCKS	Rocks formed from changes in sedimentary, igneous, or metamorphic rocks, caused by extreme heat and pressure (short of melting the rock) or contact with igneous magma.
METAMORPHOSIS	Change in the body form of an animal as it goes through its life cycle.
MITOSIS	Identical cell reproduction.
MIXTURE	Two or more substances combined physically. May be separated by physical means.
MOHO	Short for Mohorovicic discontinuity; zone separating crust from the mantle in the earth.
MOLTING	The shedding of the outer covering of skin, skeleton (arthropods), or feathers (birds).
MOMENTUM	(Mass) × (velocity) of an object equals its momentum.
MONOCOTYLEDON	Plant that produces seed which will have only *one food leaf* in the newly germinated plant.
MORAINE	Rocks deposited by glacial movement.
MOTOR NEURON	A nerve cell that carries electrical impulses from the central nervous system to a muscle or organ.
MUTANT	Cell containing non-inherited traits. These traits appear from a mutation caused by radiation or some other source.
NATURAL SELECTION	Those traits that allow organisms to compete successfully to survive.
NAUTICAL MILE	1.062 land miles.
NON-METAL	Elements that accept electrons easily in chemical reactions; poor conductors.

NOVA	A star that is expanding rapidly and giving off a tremendous amount of light energy.
OBLATE SPHEROID	A sphere flattened at the poles and bulging at the equator (shape of the earth).
OHM	Unit of electrical resistance.
OLFACTORY	Having to do with smell.
OOZE	Fine sediments found on the sea floor.
ORBIT	Path of a body that revolves about another body (e^- around a nucleus, earth around the sun).
ORGAN	A group of tissues that perform certain functions.
ORGANIC	Relating to C compounds; hydrocarbons.
OSMOSIS	The movement of H_2O through a membrane from an area of high concentration to an area of less concentration.
OSSIFICATION	The change from cartilage to bone.
OVARY	Female reproductive organ.
OVIPAROUS	Relating to egg-laying animals.
OXIDATION	The process by which oxygen combines with other substances.
PARASITE	A living organism that is dependent upon another living organism for its food.
PASCAL'S PRINCIPLE	Pressure in a confined fluid acts equally in all directions.
PENUMBRA	Partial shadow caused by an eclipse.
PERIGEE	The point at which an orbiting satellite is closest to the earth.
PERMEABLE ROCK	Rock that has enough interconnected pore spaces so as to allow H_2O to pass through it.
pH	The H^+ ion count present in a solution. Range 1-14; 1-6.9 is acid ($H^+ > OH^-$), 7.0 is neutral ($H^+ = OH^-$), 7.1 - 14 is base ($OH^- > H^+$).
PLASTIC	A material that can be shaped while soft.
PLATE	A block of crustal rock (basalt-granite) which sits on top of the asthenosphere.
POLYMER	A compound formed by two simpler compounds.
POTENTIAL ENERGY	Energy of position.
PRECIPITATE	A product that settles out of solution during a chemical reaction.
PRIME MERIDIAN	0° longitude passes through Greenwich, England.
PROMINENCE	A large solar flare that erupts from the sun's surface.
PROTEIN	Foods made of C, O, H, and N.
PSYCHROMETER	An instrument that is used to determine relative humidity.
PTYALIN	An enzyme that changes starch to sugar.
PULSAR	A star that varies regularly in brightness.

QUANTUM	An elemental unit of energy.
QUASAR	Quasi-stellar radio source.
RADIOSONDE	Weather instrumentation package sent up in a balloon.
RAIN GAUGE	A collecting device that measures rainfall.
RECEPTOR	A group of cells that receive a stimulus.
REDUCTION	The removal of oxygen from a compound.
REGENERATION	The formation of new body parts.
RELATIVE HUMIDITY	The percentage of H_2O vapor in the air at a particular temperature.
RESPIRATION	The exchange of gases in cells.
RIBOSOME	An organelle in cells where proteins are produced.
RNA	Ribonucleic acid. Carries directions to various parts of the cell as directed by the DNA.
SALT	A compound formed by a (+) and (-) ion. The ions are *not* H^+ or OH^-.
SAPROPHYTE	An organism that obtains its food from non-living organic matter.
SATELLITE	Any body revolving around another body.
SEDIMENTARY ROCKS	Rocks formed from clastic, organic, or chemical precipitates or evaporites.
SEED	A plant embryo.
SEISMOLOGY	Study of earthquakes.
SELF-POLLINATION	Process in which pollen from one plant ultimately fertilizes ova of the *same* plant.
SENSORY NEURON	Part of the nerve that carries electrical impulses.
SEXTANT	An instrument used to determine the altitude of a celestial body.
SEXUAL REPRODUCTION	Reproduction involving sperm and egg.
SMOG	Mixture of air, pollutants (i.e. smoke) and fog.
SOLAR WIND	Particles that travel away from the sun's surface.
SOLSTICE	The northernmost or southernmost advance of the vertical rays of the sun (summer, northern hemisphere, 23 1/2 °N; winter, northern hemisphere, 23 1/2 °S).
SOLUTE	The dissolved substance in a solution.
SOLUTION	A mixture of two or more substances.
SOLVENT	The dissolving medium.
SPECIES	A group of living organisms that have the same characteristics and reproduce with each other.
SPECIFIC GRAVITY	Ratio of the weight of a substance to the weight of an equal volume of H_2O.

SPECTROSCOPE	An instrument used to split white light into the colors of the rainbow (Remember the acronym, ROY G. BIV—red, orange, yellow, green, blue, indigo, and violet).
SPERM	A male reproductive cell.
STALACTITE	Mass of calcite hanging from the ceiling of a cave.
STALAGMITE	Mass of calcite on a cave floor building up under a stalactite.
STP	Standard temperature and pressure; 760 mm of Hg (1atm) and 0°C.
SUBLIME	Changing from the solid physical state to the gaseous physical state without passing through the liquid phase.
SUCRASE	An enzyme that changes sucrose to glucose.
SUPERPOSITION	Younger rocks lie on top of older rocks.
SYMBIOSIS	Two organisms that live together in order to survive.
SYNAPSE	The space between nerve endings.
SYNTHETIC	Man-made.
SYSTEM	A group of organs performing similar function.
TALUS	Rock material at the foot of a cliff.
TERRESTRIALS	Land-living organisms.
TESTES	Male reproductive organ.
THERMOCLINE	Layer of H_2O separation warm and cold water regions in a large body of H_2O.
TIME MERIDIAN	Meridian located at the center of a time zone.
TRACHEA	Air tube in terrestrial arthropods and part of the air passageway in air-breathing vertebrates.
TRANSFER RNA	T-RNA. Fashioned from M-RNA blueprint, T-RNA attracts and connects amino acids to form proteins.
TRANSFORMER	A device that changes the amount of voltage in a circuit.
TRENCH	A deep depression on the ocean floor.
TSUNAMI	A tidal wave generated by earthquakes.
UMBRA	The dark shadow caused by an eclipse.
UNIFORMITARIANISM	Understanding the present is the key to understanding the past.
UREA	A nitrogen waste product formed from used proteins.
VASCULAR BUNDLES	Strands of xylem and phloem found in the higher plants.
VENTIFACT	A wind abraded rock.
VENTRAL	Relating to "front" or lower surface of an animal.
VESTIGIAL ORGANS	Non-functioning organs.
VILLI	Projections on the wall of the intestine which absorb nutrients.
VISCOSITY	Internal friction of a fluid.

VOLATILE	Easily vaporized.
VOLT	Unit of electrical potential difference between two points in an electric field.
VULCANIZATION	Application of heat to rubber products.
WATER SHED	An area drained by one major stream.
WATT	Unit of power; 1 amp × 1 volt = 1 W.
WEATHERING	The process of breaking up rocks by chemical and/or physical means.
WORK	(Force)(distance) = work.
X-CHROMOSOME	Sex determining chromosome. Two x chromosomes make a female. One x and one y chromosomes make a male.
ZENITH	The point in the sky directly above an observer's head.
ZYMASE	Enzyme in yeast cells that acts on sugar to produce alcohol and CO_2.

Taking the CLEP Examination in Natural Sciences

Now that you have finished the entire review section, you are ready to take a sample examination. The sample examination follows the format of the CLEP General Examination in Natural Sciences.

It is important that you take this test now. While you may have done well on each type of question in isolation in the preceding section of the book, another skill is necessary. You must practice working with a variety of questions. In effect, you need to practice "switching gears" or training your mind to go from one type of question to another in a short period of time.

The following procedure should be followed for maximum benefit:

1. Find a quiet spot where you won't be disturbed.

2. Time yourself accurately. Work 45 minutes in the physical science portion and 45 minutes in the biology test section. **Don't** quit until the time is up!

3. Use the separate answer sheet provided.

4. Use the coding system for a systematic approach to the examination.

After you finish the practice test:

1. Check your answers.

2. Review the areas in which you had difficulty.

The following tests in Biology and Physical Science are designed to test general scientific knowledge. Each test consists of four parts.

In **part one**, five choices (A through E) precede a number of questions. It is a "match the question with an answer" type test. Often, this type of question can be answered by working from the answer to the question—a reverse in normal procedure for most people. Try it! You may find that you will pick up an extra point or two.

Part two is multiple choice. In this type of question you are expected to select the best answer from the five choices offered. Usually, one or two of the choices are **not** related to the question; one or two are incorrect; and two are related and correct—**BUT**, one is a better answer than the other.

Try to eliminate answer choices so that you have two or three possible choices remaining. Your chances of answering correctly improve each time you eliminate choices.

Part three concentrates on graph, chart, and diagram interpretation. Before attempting to answer questions, be sure of the information given in the graph, chart, or diagram.

Part four is much like a reading test. I suggest you read the questions **and** the answers **before** reading the selection. This will give you a better idea of where the information is within the selection.

A very important point is that **YOU MUST NOT GUESS ANSWERS**. Guessing is self-defeating.

Each incorrect answer subtracts $\frac{1}{4}$ of a point from your total score. Guessing increases wrong answers - thus increasing the number of points subtracted from your total score. What I am suggesting to you is that you leave questions **unanswered** if you cannot reduce your choices to three or less. There is **NO** penalty for unanswered questions.

Sample Examination

BIOLOGY TEST

Time: 45 Minutes   60 Questions

PART ONE

DIRECTIONS: Each group of questions below consists of five lettered choices followed by a list of numbered phrases or sentences. For each numbered phrase or sentence select the one choice that is most closely related to it. Each choice may be used once, more than once, or not at all in each group.

Questions 1-3

    (A) centriole
    (B) ribosome
    (C) mitochondria
    (D) golgi bodies
    (E) chromosomes

1.   Found only in animal cells.

2.   Rod-shaped and involved with energy release in cells.

3.   Passes genetic information to offspring.

Questions 4-7

    (A) Aristotle
    (B) Malthus
    (C) Darwin
    (D) Lamark
    (E) Devries

4.   Involved with understanding principles of population increase.

5.   Developed the theory dealing with natural selection of living organisms.

6.   Thought life began as a result of "spontaneous generation."

7.   Stated that acquired characteristics could be inherited.

Questions 8-10

    (A) lactose
    (B) bile
    (C) amylase
    (D) pepsin
    (E) sucrase

8.   Hydrolyzes proteins in the stomach

9.   Emulsifies fat particles

10. Changes starch to maltose

Questions 11-12

    (A) coclenterata
    (B) annelida
    (C) nematoda
    (D) mollusca
    (E) arthropoda

11.   Members of this phylum have had exoskeletons made of chitin.

12.   Members of this phylum are roundworms.

Questions 13-15

    (A) telophase
    (B) metaphase
    (C) interphase
    (D) anaphase
    (E) prophase

13.   Nuclear membrane reforms

14.   Chromosomes replicate themselves

15.   Chromosomes migrate to poles

Questions 16-18

    (A) fruit
    (B) fungus
    (C) gymnosperm
    (D) flower
    (E) monocot

16.   Yeast

17.   Cucumber

18.   Anther

PART TWO

DIRECTIONS: Each of the questions or incomplete statements below is followed by five suggested answers or completions. Select the one that is best in each case.

19. An organism has 36 chromosomes. How many chromosomes does each parent contribute to his offspring?

    (A) 9
    (B) 4
    (C) 12
    (D) 18
    (E) 36

20. The structure which includes all the others is:

    (A) ovary
    (B) ovule
    (C) style
    (D) pistil
    (E) stigma

21. Which of the following formula represents a simple carbohydrate?

    (A) $C_6H_{12}O_6$
    (B) $CO(NH_2)_2$
    (C) H_2SO_4
    (D) $C_{10}H_6Cl_2$
    (E) $C_6H_{10}O_3N_2$

22. An AXON is part of a:

    (A) muscle cell
    (B) nerve cell
    (C) bone cell
    (D) blood cell
    (E) skin cell

23. The correct order of structures through which air passes is:

    I.   nasal cavity
    II. bronchi
    III. larynx
    IV. air sacs
    V.   trachea

    (A) I, V, III, II, IV
    (B) I, V, III, IV, II
    (C) I, III, V, II, IV
    (D) I, III, V, IV, II
    (E) III, II, V, I, IV

24. A newly germinated plant does not need food immediately because:

    (A) it can survive for 250 hours without food
    (B) it obtains all its energy requirements through respiration and transpiration
    (C) it survives on food stored in the seed
    (D) food can be obtained only through photosynthesis
    (E) the parents nourish the young plant

25. Plants that live on dead organic matter are said to be:

    (A) parasites
    (B) saprophytes
    (C) scavengers
    (D) symbiotic
    (E) free living

26. The final products of protein digestion are:

    (A) amino acids
    (B) fatty acids
    (C) starches
    (D) sugars
    (E) vitamins

27. An oyster is closely related to:

    (A) earthworm
    (B) shark
    (C) snail
    (D) jellyfish
    (E) sponge

28. Only one of the following contains chlorophyll:

    (A) sponges
    (B) mammals
    (C) bread molds
    (D) algae
    (E) yeast

29. Of the following, which represents a homozygous condition?

    (A) Dd
    (B) DT
    (C) DD
    (D) Dt
    (E) Tt

30. The stage of development in which human characteristics become obvious is:

    (A) fetus
    (B) zygote
    (C) embryo
    (D) ovum
    (E) fertilized egg

31. If the DNA code is G-A-C, the m-RNA code is:

   (A) C-T-G
   (B) U-T-A
   (C) C-U-G
   (D) T-U-A
   (E) G-U-C

32. Sex-linked characteristics are determined by genes located on:

   (A) non-sex chromosomes
   (B) the X chromosome
   (C) the Y chromosome
   (D) both X and Y chromosomes
   (E) none of the above

33. Because of structural similarities, birds are thought to have evolved from the:

   (A) mammals
   (B) sponges
   (C) protozoans
   (D) reptiles
   (E) amphibians

34. Mammals first appeared during the:

   (A) Paleozoic
   (B) Archeozoic
   (C) Mesozoic
   (D) Cenozoic
   (E) Precambrian

35. The pancreas secretes:

   (A) bile
   (B) estrogen
   (C) insulin
   (D) thyroxin
   (E) iodine

36. A term used for the pairing of homologous chromosomes in the process of meiosis is:

   (A) coupling
   (B) synthesis
   (C) matching
   (D) replication
   (E) synapsis

37. Nitrogen is found in:

   (A) starch
   (B) protein
   (C) sugar
   (D) fat
   (E) all of the above

38. A deficiency of vitamin A may cause:

    (A) mumps
    (B) hypoglycemia
    (C) diabetes
    (D) scurvy
    (E) nightblindness

39. In the struggle for survival, those that survive are the:

    (A) largest
    (B) fittest
    (C) heaviest
    (D) fastest
    (E) strongest

40. Which blood type is called the "universal donor"?

    (A) O
    (B) A
    (C) AB
    (D) B
    (E) B negative

41. Skin is formed by:

    (A) mesoderm
    (B) ectoderm
    (C) blastocoel
    (D) endoderm
    (E) mesoglea

42. If brown eyes are dominant over blue eyes, what percentage of the offspring with brown eyes may one expect if a hybrid brown-eyed male married a blue-eyed female?

    (A) 0%
    (B) 25%
    (C) 50%
    (D) 75%
    (E) 100%

43. DNA is made of two strands of units called:

    (A) purines
    (B) pyrimidines
    (C) nucleotides
    (D) TPN
    (E) ATP/ADP

PART THREE

Questions 44-45

The following table records the results from an exercise that dealt with the effects of competition for food within a yeast cell population. Each yeast population culture was analyzed three times to determine population size.

	1 day old	2 days old	3 days old	4 days old	5 days old
1st count	115	210	530	250	150
2nd count	95	185	480	200	140
3rd count	120	261	439	180	130
Total	330	654	1449	630	420

44. In which day did the population size become so great as to force the yeast cells to compete for available food?

    (A) 1st
    (B) 2nd
    (C) 3rd
    (D) 4th
    (E) 5th

45. What was the average maximum population achieved?

    (A) 140
    (B) 218
    (C) 420
    (D) 483
    (E) 1449

46. The "y" axis is used to indicate the number of yeast cells in the population. The "x" axis indicates the age (days) of the culture. Which of the following best represents the data from the chart?

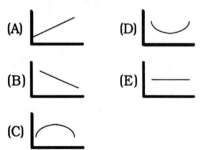

96

The following data represents data obtained in the determination of dominance and recessiveness:

	RR	Rr	rr
Tally marks	++++ ++++ ++++ ++++ 1111	++++ ++++ ++++ ++++ ++++ ++++ ++++ ++++ ++++ ++++	++++ ++++ ++++ ++++ ++++ 1
Totals	24	50	26

Genotype   = RR : Rr : rr
               24 : 50 : 26

Phenotype = Red :White
               74 : 26

47. What percentage of 100 offspring may be predicted to show the dominant trait?

    (A) 0%
    (B) 24%
    (C) 50%
    (D) 74%
    (E) 26%

48. What are the chances of getting a white trait from the cross of Rr and Rr?

    (A) 3 to 1
    (B) 1 to 4
    (C) 2 to 5
    (D) 1 to 3
    (E) 1 to 1

49. If additional data were collected, what may be predicted?

    (A) the genotype ratio would be the same
    (B) the majority selection would be "rr"
    (C) the majority selection would be "RR"
    (D) the results would be totally unpredictable
    (E) more data would be needed

Questions 50-52

Gregor Mendel was an Austrian monk who, in the 1800's, developed three theories in genetics. The ideas are summarized as follows:

I. Law of Unit Characters = each characteristic of an organism is controlled by a unit (later called a gene) inherited from an individual's parents. These units occur in pairs. One of these units may be dominant over the other.

II. Law of Independent Assortment = each inherited unit (gene) is not influenced by any others. Traits are expressed independently.

III. Law of Segregation = when an individual's sex cells are being formed, the units (genes) controlling traits separate randomly and are passed from generation to generation.

50. The two traits for eye color and nose shape:

   (A) are dependent upon each other
   (B) are inherited separately
   (C) are an expression of the same gene
   (D) were studied by Gregor Mendel
   (E) none of the above

51. If genes occur in the general population, the following would be true no matter what generation:

   (A) the genes would occur in pairs
   (B) genes separate in definite patterns
   (C) genes for one trait are dependent on other genes
   (D) genes for one characteristic double in the individual sex cells
   (E) dominance would appear in a recessive pair

52. A person with brown eyes may:

   (A) have offspring with brown eyes
   (B) have only blue-eyed offspring
   (C) have only brown-eyed offspring
   (D) have only green-eyed offspring
   (E) have offspring with any-colored eyes

Questions 53-57

Development

Development is the process by which cells that are contributed by the organism's parents grow into complete new individuals. The first stage of development is **cleavage**. The **zygote** (fertilized egg) undergoes mitotic divisions to form a ball of cells. The cell number usually doubles for the first 8 to 10 divisions, then it will be an irregular number. The solid mass of cells forms a **morula**. (The amount of yolk found in different organisms' eggs will vary.) The next stage deals with formation of the **blastula**. The morula becomes hollow and is filled with fluid. This temporary cavity is referred to as the **blastocoel** and allows room for infoldings. The blastulas differ from organism to organism. The **gastrula** is formed when cells on one side of the embryo push into the blastula cavity. Gradually the gastrula will become the cavity of the digestive system. Now the germ layer (primary cell layers) will develop. These layers (**ectoderm**, **mesoderm**, and **endoderm**) will later form the tissues of all the body structures. The ectoderm (outer layer) will eventually form nails, tooth enamel, skin, hair, nervous system, and brain. The middle layer leads to development of the bones, muscles, kidneys, circulatory and reproductive systems. The bladder, lungs, and lining of the digestive system are formed by the endoderm (inner layer).

53. Which cavity is impermanent and allows room for later indentations necessary to continued growth?

   (A) morula
   (B) gastrula
   (C) ectoderm
   (D) blastocoel
   (E) zygote

54. If the fertilized egg has 2,048 cells after a number of mitotic divisions, the next division will result in:

   (A) 2,048 cells
   (B) 3,072 cells
   (C) 4,096 cells
   (D) 8,192 cells
   (E) cannot be determined

55. The blood vessels and ovaries are formed by the:

   (A) endoderm
   (B) morula
   (C) mesoderm
   (D) zygote
   (E) ectoderm

56. Immediately upon penetration of the egg by the smaller sperm cell, which of the following is formed?

   (A) morula
   (B) zygote
   (C) gastrocoel
   (D) blastula
   (E) cleavage

57. Of the following combinations, which two deal with the same body system (cavity and lining)?

   (A) gastrula - endoderm
   (B) blastula - endoderm
   (C) gastrula - mesoderm
   (D) morula - gastrula
   (E) gastrula - ectoderm

Questions 58-60

Evolution

There are two types of evolution - convergent and divergent. Divergent evolution is also referred to as adaptive radiation. Two structures become increasingly different as a result of evolutionary changes. An example of this would be the arm of man and the flipper of a whale. Because they are of common ancestry, they are both vertebrates and the structures have highly specialized functions. They are termed homologous.

Animals that have structures that are similar in form and function are the result of convergent evolution. An example of this would be the porpoise (a fairly recently evolved mammal) and some of the extinct aquatic reptiles. They both have similar body shapes and the same fish-eating habits. Their structures are considered to be analogous (like function, different origin).

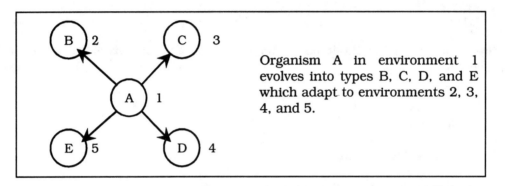

Organism A in environment 1 evolves into types B, C, D, and E which adapt to environments 2, 3, 4, and 5.

58. The structure in the diagram are the results of which kind of evolution?

   (A) divergent
   (B) convergent
   (C) both (A) and (B)
   (D) neither (A) nor (B)
   (E) cannot be determined

59. Which of the following cannot be determined by the diagram?

   (A) A, B, C, D, and E are different organisms
   (B) the environments are at least slightly different
   (C) organisms B and C are descendants of organism A
   (D) organisms B, C, D, and E have analogous structures
   (E) organisms B, C, D, and E have homologous structures

60. Which of the following pairs are **not** indicative of homologous structures?

   (A) man's arm - bird wing
   (B) fly wing - bat wing
   (C) whale flipper - bat wing
   (D) mole forelimb - man's arm
   (E) man's arm - salamander forelimb

100

PHYSICAL SCIENCE TEST

Time: 45 minutes

60 Questions

PART ONE

DIRECTIONS: Each group of questions below consists of five lettered choices followed by a list of numbered phrases or sentences. For each numbered phrase or sentence select the one choice that is most closely related to it. Each choice may be used once, more than once, or not at all in each group.

Questions 1-4

(A) $2\,KClO_3 \rightarrow 2\,KCl + 3O_2$
(B) $H_2\,SO_3 \rightarrow H_2O + SO_2$
(C) $Zn + CuSO_4 \rightarrow ZnSO_4 + Cu$
(D) $NaCl + AgNO_3 \rightarrow NaNO_3 + AgCl$
(E) $Xe + O_2 \rightarrow XeO$

Which of the above represents:

1.   A single replacement reaction?

2.   A decomposition of a chlorate?

3.   A double replacement?

4.   An inert element which will **not** enter into a reaction and therefore, example given is wrong.

Questions 5-6

(A) electron
(B) proton
(C) nucleus
(D) neutron
(E) atomic weight

5.   Which of the above is transferred from one atom to another when an ionic bond is formed?

6.   Which part of the atom may undergo fission or fusion?

Questions 7-8

(A) Coastal Plain
(B) Plateau
(C) Coastal Range
(D) Shield
(E) Interior Plains

The following fall into which physiographic province?

7.   Southern Canada

8.   Eastern Oregon

Questions 9-11

    (A) Copernicus
    (B) Ptolemy
    (C) Kepler
    (D) Galileo
    (E) Newton

9. Set the sun at the center of the Solar System.

10. Used Tycho Brahe's data to interpret planetary motion.

11. Developed the laws governing planetary motion.

Questions 12-14

    (A) absorption spectra
    (B) continuous spectra
    (C) emission spectra
    (D) line spectra
    (E) solar spectrum

12. Each chemical substance has its own characteristic spectra.

13. Interruptions by dark lines in a spectra.

14. Fraunhofer lines

Questions 15-17

    (A) nimbostratus
    (B) altostratus
    (C) cumulus
    (D) cirrus
    (E) cumulonimbus

15. Typical "thunder shower" clouds

16. Thin, wispy high clouds

17. Fair weather clouds

PART TWO

DIRECTIONS: Each of the questions or incomplete statements below is followed by five suggested answers or completions. Select the one that is best in each case.

18. Archeopteryx is:

    (A) an ancient fish
    (B) giant fern existing in the late Triassic
    (C) a shellfish used as an index fossil
    (D) an amblypod
    (E) the oldest known bird

19. The following diagram is:

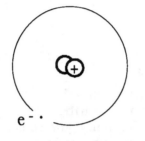

    (A) heavy hydrogen
    (B) helium
    (C) a nucleus
    (D) uranium
    (E) lithium

20. ▼▼▼ is a symbol for:

    (A) a warm front
    (B) a cold front
    (C) thunderstorms
    (D) a stationary front
    (E) an occluded front

21. Fossil fuels are found in:

    (A) granitic rocks
    (B) the waters of the oceans
    (C) igneous rocks
    (D) metamorphic rocks
    (E) sedimentary rocks

22. Which of the following is different from the others?

    (A) H_2O
    (B) O_2
    (C) Cl_2
    (D) $CaCl_2$
    (E) SO_3

23. An astronaut weighs 150 pounds before blasting off to the Moon. What happens to the astronaut's weight as he leaves the earth?

(A) It increases until he reaches a point where the earth and moon gravitation are equal.
(B) It increases - twice the distance = twice the weight.
(C) It remains the same throughout the whole trip.
(D) It decreases - twice the distance = half of his original weight.

(E) It decreases as his distance increases by a factor of $\dfrac{1}{d^2}$

24. Ocean currents are affected mainly by:

(A) salinity
(B) temperature
(C) winds
(D) earth's rotation
(E) all of the above

25. The highest tides occur when:

(A) the Moon is closest to the Earth
(B) the Moon is farthest from the Earth
(C) the Moon, Sun and Earth fall in line with each other
(D) the Earth, Moon, and Sun form a right angle with each other
(E) during the summer months

26. A supernova is related to all but one of the following:

(A) cepheid variable
(B) quasar
(C) eclipsing binary
(D) white dwarf
(E) red giant

27. The sun produces energy by:

(A) nuclear fusion
(B) atomic fission
(C) ordinary chemical reactions
(D) burning its fuel
(E) giving off heat

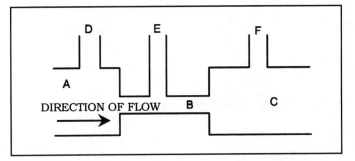

A,B,C represent velocity of the liquid.
D,E,F represent pressure supporting a liquid column.

28. The velocity and pressure at B and E is:

    (A) lower than A and C and lower than D and F
    (B) lower than A, higher than C; lower than D, higher than F
    (C) remains constant throughout the system
    (D) higher than A and C, lower than D and F
    (E) higher than A, lower than C; higher than D, lower than F

29. The mathematical expression of Ohm's Law is:

    (A) $E = IR$
    (B) $P = IE$
    (C) $E = MC^2$
    (D) $F \times d = W$
    (E) $M \times V = D$

30. The difference between a solid and a liquid of the same substance is:

    (A) the size of the matter
    (B) the kinetic energy each possesses
    (C) the shape of the container
    (D) the potential energy of the matter
    (E) the mass of the substance

31. Earthquake waves traveling through the earth indicate:

    (A) four major regions—crust, mantle, core and outer core
    (B) three major regions—crust, mantle and core
    (C) two major regions—exterior and interior
    (D) no regions at all! The earth is solid throughout
    (E) many different regions which change position from time-to-time

32. A compound is found to contain 75% C and 25% H_2 by weight. What is the empirical formula for this compound?

    at. wt. C = 12, H = 1

    (A) CH_2
    (B) C_3H
    (C) CH
    (D) CH_4
    (E) carbon and hydrogen do not react.

33. The type of bedrock found on the seafloor is:

(A) granite
(B) limestone
(C) clay
(D) pegmatite
(E) basalt

34. The planet with the most eccentric orbit is:

(A) Mercury
(B) Earth
(C) Jupiter
(D) Uranus
(E) Pluto

35. The age of the Earth is estimated to be:

(A) 10 billion years
(B) 186,000 years
(C) 4,500,000,000 years
(D) 93,000 years
(E) 8,000 years

36. The magnetosphere around the Earth is:

(A) uniform in shape
(B) larger in size at the poles than at the equator
(C) is distorted by the solar wind
(D) captures ultra-violet rays from the sun
(E) is largely dependent upon the weather

37. A certain volume of gas undergoes an increase in temperature and the pressure remains constant.

(A) the volume will decrease
(B) the volume will increase
(C) the volume remains the same
(D) the volume will increase until the final temperature is met, and then the volume will decrease slightly
(E) temperature changes only pressure, not volume

38. Air pollution is greatest when:

(A) it is windy and cold
(B) a temperature inversion occurs
(C) it is warm and windy
(D) power plants are operating at maximum
(E) entrophication occurs

39. The crust of the Earth is composed mainly of:

(A) Si and O_2
(B) Fe and O_2
(C) Fe and Mg
(D) H_2 and O_2
(E) carbon

PART THREE

Questions 40-41, use the following diagram:

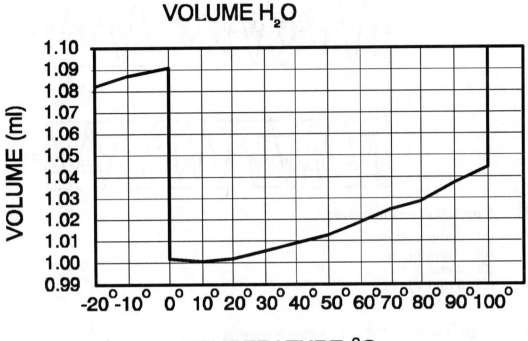

VOLUME H₂O

The above graph represents the volume of H_2O at varying temperatures.

40. The state of H_2O at 0° is:

   (A) all H_2O
   (B) all ice
   (C) in a phase change from ice-to-water
   (D) in a phase change from water-to-gas
   (E) gas

41. The volume of the water changing to gas at 100° C will:

   (A) increase slightly
   (B) increase greatly
   (C) remain constant
   (D) decrease slightly
   (E) decrease greatly

Questions 42-44

Below are two typical wave pattern representations.

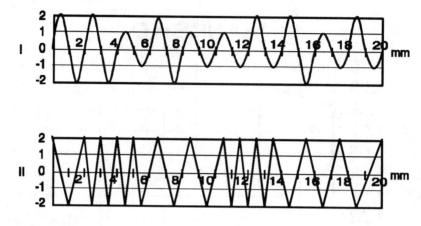

42. Rarefaction occurs between:

   (A) 2 and 4, #I
   (B) 0 and 14, #I
   (C) 2 and 4, #II
   (D) 5 and 10, #II
   (E) 10 and 13, #II

43. Of the above, an FM radio signal is most like:

   (A) #I, because FM depends upon amplitude variation
   (B) #I, because FM depends upon frequency constant
   (C) combinations of #I and #II
   (D) #II, because FM depends upon keeping the amplitude constant
   (E) #II, because AM is used commercially

44. The wavelength of the wave in #II is:

   (A) about 1 mm
   (B) about 4 mm
   (C) about 6 mm
   (D) about 14 mm
   (E) more information is needed to determine the wavelength

Use this graph to answer question 45:

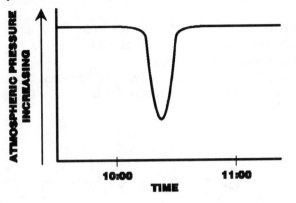

45. The above drop in air pressure might indicate:

    (A) thunderstorms
    (B) hurricane
    (C) tornado
    (D) a snowstorm
    (E) fair weather

Questions 46-48

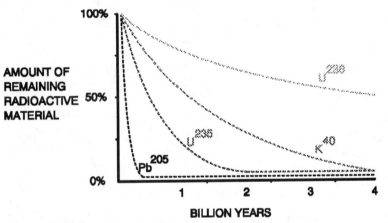

46. After two half-lives,:

    (A) 50% of the U^{235} remains
    (B) 75% of the U^{235} remains
    (C) 25% of the U^{235} remains
    (D) U^{235} is "used up"
    (E) 98% of the U^{235} is used up

47. How many half-lives must U^{235} go through before 99% of it has decayed?

    (A) two half-lives
    (B) three half-lives
    (C) four half-lives
    (D) five half-lives
    (E) seven half-lives

48.   Radioactive elements are useful for "dating" events. The reason this dating method is reliable is:

(A)   radioactive elements are abundant in all rocks
(B)   disintegration takes place at a constant rate
(C)   radioactivity speeds up with time
(D)   radioactivity separates the Eras of the Geologic Time Scale
(E)   it works well with old as well as recent fossils

Questions 49-50

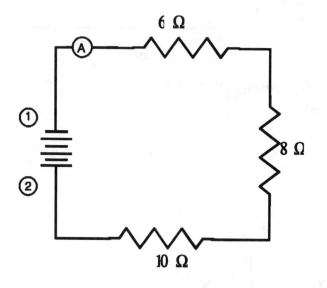

49. |ı|ı|ı is a:

(A)   resistor
(B)   ammeter
(C)   power source
(D)   voltmeter
(E)   rheostat

50.   If the current in the circuit is 0.5 amps, what is the total voltage 1 through 2?

(A)   12 volts
(B)   24 volts
(C)   48 volts
(D)   6 volts
(E)   0.5 volts

Questions 51-52

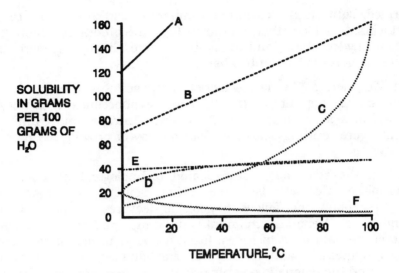

51. As the temperature increases, the solubility decreases for substance:

(A) A
(B) B
(C) C
(D) E
(E) F

52. The substance with the greatest affinity to dissolve as the temperature increases is:

(A) F
(B) E
(C) D
(D) C
(E) B

PART FOUR

As the earth formed, light silica rock-forming minerals rose to the surface of the earth and formed the continents. It is likely that, on the surface, the processes which gave the planet its unique atmosphere, hydrosphere, and lithosphere, were already in operation. As billions of years passed, these spheres evolved into what they are today.

In 1915, Alfred Wegener, a German scientist, proposed his theory of Continental Drift. Wegener noticed the unique "fit" of the jig-saw-like shorelines of Africa/South America, Africa/Europe, and to a lesser degree, North America/Europe, and came to the conclusion that the continents were "drifting apart". He had no way of proving his theory given the then present technology.

With the advent of the space-age, sophisticated technological data gathering procedures became common-place. Geo-scientists interpreting seismological data began correlating unrelated data to explain the following geologic features or phenomena: earthquakes, volcanoes, island arcs, trenches, mountain building, mid-ocean ridges, and sea-floor spreading. Some of the data used includes: fossil correlation, age of sea-floor sediments and continents, depth frequency, and location of earthquakes, location of volcanoes/island arcs/and trenches, and the magnetic polarity orientation on either side of mid-ocean ridges.

53. The name of the present day theory explaining continental drift is:

    (A) protoplanet hypothesis
    (B) plate tectonics
    (C) continental drift theory
    (D) isostasy
    (E) geosynclinal theory

54. Accretion of the earth was probably complete:

    (A) after differentiation and solidification occurred
    (B) after the formation of the hydrosphere
    (C) during differentiation of earth materials
    (D) before the sun became a star
    (E) after solidification occurred

55. Much of the data above was gathered from what area?

    (A) stratigraphy of the Grand Canyon
    (B) San Andreas fault
    (C) Hawaii
    (D) North American east coast
    (E) the "ring of fire"

56. The "driving" force moving the continents is thought to be convection cells in the earth's lower crust and upper mantle. What supplies the energy for the driving force?

    (A) the sun
    (B) original heat left over from the earth's "hot" origin
    (C) heat energy from radioactive decay
    (D) friction generated by the crust rubbing against the mantle
    (E) gravitational attraction between surface and interior

The following information is about the planet Venus.

Size	a few miles smaller than earth
Surface Temperature	600° + C
Atmospheric Composition	CO_2 , some H_2O, some H_2SO_4 droplets
Atmospheric Pressure	100× earth's at the surface
Revolution	about 220 days
Rotation	Retrograde, 240 days
Magnetic Field	none
Gravity Field	about the same as earth

57. A "day" on Venus is:

(A) 220 earth days
(B) longer than a "day" on earth
(C) 24 hours
(D) $\frac{1}{240}$ of a rotation
(E) less than a "day" on earth

58. The reason Venus is extremely warm is:

(A) it is the planet closest to the sun
(B) it has no clouds to shield it from insolation
(C) the "greenhouse effect"
(D) volcanic activity warms the atmosphere
(E) original heat from Venus' creation warms the surface of the planet

59. Some scientists think Venus may be a "captured" planet. Of the above data, which fact would lend itself to support that idea?

(A) its atmospheric composition
(B) its temperature
(C) it has no satellites
(D) it is approximately the same size as earth
(E) its retrograde rotation

60. The reason for the high atmospheric pressure is probably:

(A) atmospheric density
(B) the frequent dust storms on the surface
(C) abnormally high gravity field
(D) absence of a magnetic field
(E) the solar wind pressure

Answers Sample Examination—Biology

1. (A) Centrioles are found in animal cells. They are cytoplasmic bodies which duplicate and divide early in cell division.

2. (C) The mitochondria store and release energy within the cell utilizing the ADP-ATP cycle.

3. (E) The genes which determine an organism's traits are found on the chromosomes.

4. (B) A 19th century political economist who pointed out that food production could not keep up with the geometric increase of world population.

5. (C) Darwin's idea that certain organisms of a species possess characteristics that allow them to survive while others of the same species that do **not** possess these characteristics have less of a chance of surviving.

6. (A) Aristotle organized biological knowledge in ancient Greece. Much of what he **thought** was fact, in time, became questionable. One of these facts was "spontaneous generation"—life springing from certain non-living or dead organisms.

7. (D) Lamark explained certain characteristics, once learned, were passed on to future generations; also, that learned characteristics would disappear through non-use in future generations.

8. (D) Pepsin is an enzyme in the stomach that changes proteins to peptones and proteoses.

9. (B) Secreted by the liver and stored in the gall bladder, bile increases the digestive action of lipase by breaking large globules of fat into smaller droplets. These droplets are in a colloidal suspension called an emulsion.

10. (C) Amylase in the small intestine continues the action begun by ptyalin in the mouth, of breaking down starches into simpler sugars.

11. (E) Arthropods (spiders, lobsters, grasshoppers, centipedes) have hard outer body skeletons made of chitin. The other selections are mainly soft-bodies.

12. (C) Roundworms are **Nematodes**. Segmented worms are **Annelids** and flatworms are **Platyhelminthes** (not a choice).

13. (A) The nuclear membrane reforms after the migration of chromosomes to the poles of what will shortly be daughter cells. This occurs during **telophase** in mitosis.

14. (C) During the so-called "resting period" the cell is very active. Besides growing larger, the cell is occupied with reproducing the DNA (chromosome) material.

15. (D) Migration occurs during the **Anaphase** stage of mitosis.

16. (B) Yeast is a common fungus growth. Yeasts multiply rapidly under ideal conditions. If, however, conditions become unfavorable, yeasts survive by forming an ascus and become dormant until conditions again become favorable.

17. (A) A cucumber is a modified berry. It has a hard outer covering around a fleshy, watery ovary and contains many seeds.

18. (D)   The anther is part of the flower part called the **stamen**. It is a knob-like end portion which produces pollen.

19. (D)   In sexual reproduction, each parent contributes one-half of the total number of chromosomes needed to make a normal organism. The process of producing sex cells is called **meiosis** and it is a reduction process. In this example, each parent would produce a sex cell with one of each kind of chromosome—this is known as a **haploid number of chromosomes** (abbreviated: [n]). Cells other than sex cells contain a **diploid** number of chromosomes (2n).

20. (D)   The **pistil** is composed of an ovary containing the ovule at its base, the style, located between the **stigma** (top) and the ovary (base).

21. (A)   Carbohydrates are composed of carbon, oxygen, and hydrogen. Sugars would have higher subscript numbers.

22. (B)   Axons are the part of the nerve cell that carry impulses **away** from the nerve body.

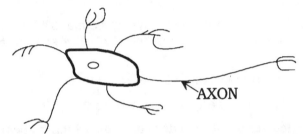

23. (C)   Air passes through the nose (nasal cavity, I), past the larynx (back of the throat, III), through the trachea (V), separating into either bronchus (II), finally into the **alveoli** (air sacs, IV).

24. (C)   The monocots and dicots have one and two food seeds respectively, which provide the plant with food until food-producing leaves grow.

25. (B)   Saprophytic plants and bacteria account for the removal, or decay, of dead organisms from the surface of the earth.

26. (A)   The final products of protein digestion are amino acids—an energy-releasing process.

27. (C)   Both are mollusks.

28. (D)   The algae are the only **green** plants of the choices.

29. (C)   Choices (A), (D), and (E) represent heterozygous pairs. Choice (B) is a mixed pair.

30. (A)   It is during fetal development that human characteristics first appear. Choices (B) and (E) are the same and represent only **one** cell. An ovum (D) is an unfertilized egg. An embryo (C) is the stage of development just prior to becoming a fetus.

31. (C)   The corresponding pair-ups are:

> guanine—cytosine (C)
> adenine—uracil (U)
> cytosine—guanine (G)

32. (B)   If a pair of x chromosomes is present in the organism, the sex is female. If only **one** x chromosome is present, the sex of the organism is **male**.

33. (D) The first birds (archeopteryx) had teeth and scaly skin like their reptile contemporaries.

34. (C) It is thought by some scientists that the appearance of mammals during the Mesozoic Era caused the downfall of the reptiles that dominated the earth (about 250 million years ago).

35. (C) Insulin is the chief regulator of the breakdown of sugars in tissues. Bile is secreted by the liver; thyroxin by the thyroid gland; and estrogen is secreted by the ovaries.

36. (E) The term "synapsis" is given to this action. Only coupling (A) could be substituted; however, biologically (E) is a better choice.

37. (B) Starches, fats, and sugars contain carbon, **hydrogen, and oxygen**. Only proteins contain C, H, O, and **nitrogen**.

38. (E) Other symptoms of Vitamin A deficiency are: retarded growth, bad teeth, poor skin condition.

    Mumps (A) is a viral infection. Hypoglycemia (B) is controlled by insulin—diabetes. (C) is the lack of insulin to metabolize sugars. Scurvy is a Vitamin C deficiency.

39. (B) The basis of Natural Selection as presented by Darwin.

40. (A) "O" may donate blood to any other blood type.

41. (B) Skin originates from the ectodermal cells which appear during gastrulation. Mesoderm (A) and endoderm (D) form other "inside" tissues and organs in humans. Mesoglea (E) is found in sponges and is the step between two germ layers and three germ layers (evolution). A blastocoel is the cavity in the hollow blastula.

42. (C) A brown-eyed male (hybrid) Bb crosses with a blue-eyed female (homozygous) bb.

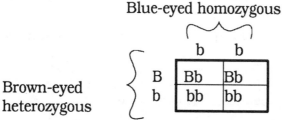

43. (C) ATP/ADP (E) are phosphate compounds involved with energy release and storage. TPN (D) is also involved with the above process. (A) and (B) are parts that make up a nucleotide. A nucleotide is at least a three-part unit of DNA.

44. (C) The chart clearly shows that the third day was critical between the population and the food. Therefore, the number of yeast cells drops off dramatically.

45. (D) By adding the column under "3 days," the sum 1449 is obtained. This number, divided by 3 (representing the number of "counts" done), equals 483.

46. (C) A plot of the numbers looks like this:

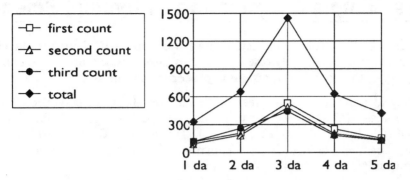

- □ first count
- △ second count
- ● third count
- ◆ total

47. (D) Red is dominant. This is seen in the chart where Rr is shown. Genotype distribution shows 24 pure reds and 50 hybrid reds. The white, which is recessive, comprises only 26 of the total data. The breakdown of percentages is seen in the phenotype: roughly 75% red—25% white.

48. (D) Rr crossed with Rr produces the following:

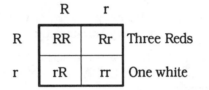

	R	r	
R	RR	Rr	Three Reds
r	rR	rr	One white

49. (A) The ratio would remain the same as long as a sufficient number were counted from a randomly selected population.

50. (B) The law of dependent assortment and segregation indicates that traits are **not** dependent upon each other and may be separated during sex cell formation.

51. (A) The Law of Dominance indicates that genes occur in pairs.

52. (E) The parents' sex cells combine—the genes (chromosomes) contain the information which will control eye color. It is a fact that brown-eyed parents have blue-eyed, gray-eyed, and green-eyed offspring—even different shades of brown. So, (E) is the best answer, although (A) is also correct.

53. (D) The blastocoel gives way to the forming **archenteron** and finally disappears.

54. (E) After a number of cell divisions have occurred (8 to 10), divisions are no longer predictable.

55. (C) Mesoderm forms the circulatory system, as well as much of the reproductive system.

56. (B) The zygote is the fertilized egg. This is the first cell from which all other cells of the organism will arise.

57. (A) The endoderm does not truly form until gastrulation occurs. The endoderm forms the cavity which later becomes the digestive system.

58. (A) The diagram radiates outward from a common point. The adaptation to the different environments from common ancestry indicates divergent evolution.

59. (D) Again, having the same origin rules out analogous structures.

60. (B) A fly is an invertebrate, while a bat is a vertebrate—arising from different origins. All other choices originate from a vertebrate background.

Answers Sample Examination—Physical Science

1. **(C)** The Zinc (Zn) Atom is more active than the Copper (Cu) and replaces the Cu in the compound. Since only **one** of the members (the metal) of the compound was exchanged, this is called a **single replacement** reaction.

2. **(A)** The key to answering this question lies in the ability to spot the CHLORATE. Of the choices, (A) and (D) contain Cl. Cl in compound form is usually a CHLO<u>RIDE</u> (metal Cl or metal Cl_2). Therefore, $KClO_3$ represents something **other than** a chloride—as **chlorate**. Also, only (A) and (B) represent **decomposition**—and only (A) contains Cl.

3. **(D)** Here, the Ag and Na change places. Since two elements are exchanged between compounds, it is classified as a **double replacement** reaction.

4. **(E)** Xe is one of the inert elements (He, Ar, Ne, **Xe**, Kr). Under ordinary circumstances, Xe will **not** enter into chemical reactions.

5. **(A)** Electrons move from one atom to another when forming an **ionic bond**.

6. **(C)** Fission is the splitting of a heavy nucleus into two or more lighter nuclei. Fusion is the formation of a heavy nucleus by combining lighter nuclei.

7. **(D)** The Canadian Shield, mainly granitoid rock, is one of the oldest rocks in the world. South of Canada, in the U.S.A., the interior plains appear and they are primarily sedimentary rock.

8. **(B)** Eastern Oregon belongs to the Columbia Plateau. Western Oregon belongs to the Coastal Range province.

9. **(A)** Copernicus, in an effort to better explain planetary movement, set the sun at the center of the solar system. Prior to this, a complicated system of planets, sun, and moon, revolved about the earth as suggested by Ptolemy many years before Copernicus. The earth-centered theory is called the **geocentric** theory. The sun-centered theory is called the **heliocentric** theory. The heliocentric theory is correct.

10. **(C)** Kepler was an assistant to Tycho. He used the data collected by Brahe to develop three ideas about planetary motion. These ideas were:

    1. all planets revolve around the sun in an ellipse with the sun at one of the centers of the ellipse.

    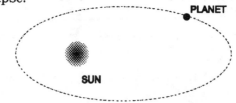

    2. Planets cover equal areas in equal time in their trip around the sun.

    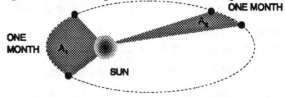

    3. The larger the orbit, the longer it takes for a planet to make one revolution.

118

11. (E) Newton developed the mathematics to explain the movement of celestial bodies.

12. (D) Elements heated to a point where they begin to glow incadescent give off characteristic colors. These color lines are like fingerprints—they always fall on the same position (wavelength line) on the A scale. As such, bright-line spectra are useful for chemical analysis.

13. (A) By passing light which would normally form a continuous spectrum through a known incandescent vaporous substances, light energy is absorbed at those particular wavelengths. This produces dark-lines where light would normally appear. These dark lines are known as **fraunhofer** lines.

14. (A) as explained in #13.

15. (E) Typical thundershower clouds are cumulonimbus. These clouds range from 2,000 ft. at the base to 20,000 ft. at the top. Violent winds moving up through the cloud carries rain up to altitudes where it freezes to form hail. The winds also set up an electrical charge difference between bodies of air or between air and surface which results in lightning and thunder.

16. (D) Cirrus are the highest (10,000-20,000 ft.) of the stratiform type clouds.

17. (C) Cumulus are the puffy, white to grey clouds seen on fair weather days.

18. (E) Archeopteryx was the first feathered animal with wings. It had a reptile-like head and mouth and was about the same size as a pigeon. Although there were other flying animals prior to Archeopteryx, it is considered to be the first bird because of the feathers. It appeared during the Jurassic period of the Mesozoic era (190 million years ago).

19. (A) The presence of one proton makes this hydrogen. Since it contains an extra particle in the nucleus (a neutron) it must be a **heavy** hydrogen having an atomic weight of 2.

    The presence of an electron rules out letter (C).

20. (B) This is the accepted symbol for a cold front.

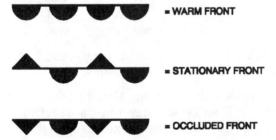

= WARM FRONT

= STATIONARY FRONT

= OCCLUDED FRONT

Thundershowers do not have a weather symbol similar to the above.

21. (E) Granite and igneous rocks, (A) and (C), have a hot, liquid beginning and do not contain fossils. Metamorphic rocks usually destroy any fossils they contain. One exception would be the metamorphosis of bituminous (soft) coal into **anthracite** (hard) coal. However, our answer requires a rock in which fuels (plural) would be contained.

    Many sedimentary rocks form in the ocean. The animals and plants that eventually become oil live in the oceans. Some sedimentary rocks form on land in swamps. Coal and associated shale beds formed this way. So, the only real answer covering all the fuels would be (E) Sedimentary rocks.

22. (D) Ca Cl$_2$ is an **ionic bond** compound. H$_2$O, O$_2$, Cl$_2$, and SO$_3$ are all in a covalent bonding condition.

23. (E) As the astronaut travels away from the earth, his weight (gravitation attraction between his mass and the mass of the earth) decreases by the square of the distance. At twice the distance from the earth, the astronaut will weigh ¼ of what he weighed at the surface.

$$(150 - d^2 = 150 \times \frac{1}{d^2} = 150 \times \frac{1}{2^2} = 150 \times \frac{1}{4} = 37.5 \text{ pounds})$$

To carry this further, twice the distance $\qquad = \dfrac{1}{2^2}$

three times the distance $\qquad = \dfrac{1}{3^2}$

four times the distance $\qquad = \dfrac{1}{4^2}$

etc.

24. (E) Ocean surface currents are subject to winds which circulate most of the water. Temperature changes cause changes in salinity—these two combined are responsible for vertical circulation. The earth's rotation causes the surface currents to bend away from their original path of travel. This deflection is known as the **coriolis effect**.

25. (C) The moon is largely responsible for the ocean tides. The distance difference between "closest" approach and "furthest" away is relatively small and does not have much bearing on the "highest" or "lowest" tides.

When the earth, moon, and sun fall into the same line, gravitational attraction between all three causes **spring tides**. These are the highest tides.

When e-m-s fall at right angles to each other, the "lowest" high tides are recorded: These tides are called **neap** tides.

26. (B) A quasar is a quasi—stellar radio source. Quasars give off large amounts of radio energy as well as light. They have a spectral "red-shift" which suggests they are moving away from earth at extremely high velocities.

27. (A) It is thought that the sun produces energy by the fusion of Hydrogen nuclei into He nuclei. In the process, matter is transformed into energy. (B) and (C) do **not** release energy in amounts comparable to the fusion reaction. (D) is a chemical reaction and (E) does not explain where the heat originated (the question).

28. (D) As the liquid goes through the narrow section B , it speeds up. That means the velocity increases. The liquid in column E is lowered.

The above phenomenon is explained using Bernouilli's principle. In a system such as above, the kinetic energy (K.E.) + the pressure is constant per unit area. Applying this, the column D and F would be higher than E because K.E. is directly proportional to velocity (higher velocity = higher K.E.). So, to keep it constant throughout the system, as the K.E. increases, the pressure decreases.

29. (A) Amperage × resistance = electromotive force (voltage), or resistance (ohms Ω) =

$$\frac{\text{voltage (volts)}}{\text{amperage (amps)}}$$

(B) is the formula for Power (Watts) in an electrical circuit.

(C) is Einstein's equation, energy = mass × (speed of light)^2

(D) is the formula for Work (force × distance = work)

(E) is the formula for density ($\frac{\text{mass}}{\text{volume}}$ = density)

30. (B) The amount of K.E. is related directly to the movement (velocity) of the substance. The more K.E. the faster the molecular movement. Gases have more K.E. than liquids. Liquids have more K.E. than solids.

Size (A), shape (C), and mass (E) have little to do with K.E.. P.E. is stored energy and is **not** part of this problem.

31. (A) **factual**

32. (D) To determine an answer, a quick calculation is in order.

$$\frac{\text{Weight \% of C}}{\text{atomic weight of C}} = \frac{75\%}{12} = 6.25$$

$$\frac{\text{Weight \% of H}}{\text{atomic weight of H}} = \frac{25\%}{1} = 25$$

The relationship between C and H is:

$$C = \frac{6.25}{6.25} = 1$$

$$H = \frac{25}{6.25} = 4 \text{ or } 1:4$$

Therefore, the empirical formula is CH_4

33. (E) Basalt is the lower layer of the crust. It is the product of quick cooling igneous magma (lava) pushed out at the mid-ocean ridges. Overlying rocks are sedimentary, having formed from either chemical, organic, or clastic origins. Limestone (B) and clay (C) are sedimentary.

Pegmatitie (D) and Granite (A) are also igneous, but texture indicates they formed deep within the crust rather than at the surface.

34. (E) Pluto has the most eccentric orbit. In a portion of its orbit it is closer to the sun than Neptune.

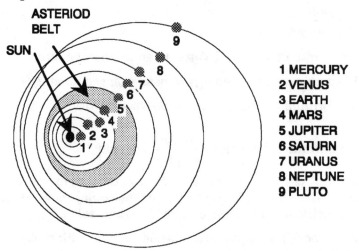

ASTERIOD BELT

SUN

1 MERCURY
2 VENUS
3 EARTH
4 MARS
5 JUPITER
6 SATURN
7 URANUS
8 NEPTUNE
9 PLUTO

35. (C) Based upon the radioactive dating of rocks on earth, meteorites, and moon rocks, a close estimate of the age of the earth is 4.5 billion years.

36. (C) The magnetosphere is distorted away from the sun side of earth by the solar wind.

SOLAR WIND   MAGNETOSPHERE

SUN   EARTH

37. (B) Charles' Law states that if pressure remains constant, the volume of a gas is directly proportional to temperature changes. So, if the temperature increases the volume increases, and if the temperature decreases the volume decreases.

38. (B) Temperature inversions occur when air masses stagnate thus trapping a warm air layer below a cold air layer. Normally, warm air rises and cold air falls to replace the warm air.

The trapped, warm air collects pollutants until rain or winds clean it out.

39. (A) Silicon and oxygen make up approximately 75% of the crust. The following diagram breaks down the **approximate** percentages.

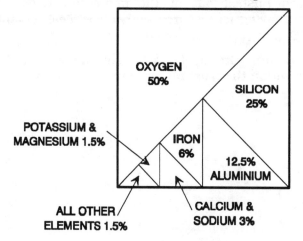

OXYGEN 50%

SILICON 25%

POTASSIUM & MAGNESIUM 1.5%

IRON 6%

12.5% ALUMINIUM

ALL OTHER ELEMENTS 1.5%

CALCIUM & SODIUM 3%

40. (C) In order for ice to change to water, it must acquire 80 calories of heat/gram. This extra heat does **not** change the temperature—only the state of the H_2O (solid to liquid). This is represented by the vertical line in the graph at O˚.

41. (B) Again, as the phase change from liquid to gas occurs, extra energy must be acquired by the water (540 cal/gram). The volume of the gaseous water will be very large by comparison. Example: steam kettles that whistle; pots whose covers rattle as the gaseous water escape.

42. (D) The wave is spread out between 5 and 10 of #II. Choices (A) and (B) do not apply since the nature of the wave is consistent in frequency. (C) shows a compression of the wave, and (D) a part of a compression and rarefaction.

43. (D) As stated in the answer F M means frequency modulation—or variation.

Choice (A) and (B) do not apply since it is not clear what type of wave (AM or FM) it represents. (C) is a possibility, but not the BEST answer. (E) is true, but the same can also be said of FM.

44. (C) Measuring from rarefaction to rarefaction, 0 mm to 6 mm, or 6 mm to 12 mm; or compression to compression, 3 mm to 9 mm, the spread is 6 mm.

45. (C) Given the duration, 10-15 minutes, only (A) and (C) are possible answers. Thunderstorms generally last longer than 10-15 minutes and are **NOT** accompanied by such a large drop in pressure. That leaves only (C) as an answer.

46. (C) Two half-lives equals $1/2 \times 1/2$ or 1/4. So, half of the U^{235} decays during the first half-life. Half of the remaining half ($1/2 \times 1/2 = 1/4$) decays during the second half-life, leaving one quarter (1/4) of the original U^{235}.

47. (E) To answer simply: $(½)^n = 99\%$ decayed.

½	x ½	x ½	x ½	x ½	x ½	x ½	
1	2	3	4	5	6	7	← half-life number
50%	25%	12.5%	6.25%	3.125%	1.5%	.075%	← % of original U^{235} remaining

So, practically speaking, U^{235} after seven half-lives is 99% decayed.

48. (B) Like a clock, radioactive decay is constant and consistency is the key factor which allows scientists to date the age of fossils or events that existed millions and millions of years ago.

49. (C) Circuits must have a power source in order to function. ⎯◊◊◊◊⎯ is (A); A is an ammeter. The voltmeter ⎯Ⓥ⎯ and rheostat ⎯◊◊◊⎯ are not shown in the diagram.

50. (A) Resistance in a series circuit is additive.

$R_1 + R_2 + R_3 = 6\Omega + 10\Omega + 8\Omega = 24\Omega$

$E = I \times R$ or Voltage = 0.5 amp $\times 24\Omega$

$E = 12$ volts

51. (E) F is the only line that decreases solubility as the temperature increases. All other choices increase in solubility as temperature increases.

52. (D) Curve C shows a change of 150 grams/85° temperature increase. Other choices show:

> (A), line F, decreases
> (B), line E, 5 grams/100° increase
> (C), line D, 25 grams/100° increase
> (E), line B, 90 grams/100° increase

53. (B) Fact.

54. (E) After solidification, it is thought that the earth heated up and differentiation of materials took place.

55. (E) The "ring of fire" circles the Pacific Ocean. It contains volcanoes, earthquake zones, trenches, and island arcs.

56. (C) It is presently thought that radioactive decay, which releases heat energy as a by-product, is responsible for the convection cells.

57. (B) A day on Venus is one rotation, 240 earth days. One Venus day = 240 earth days.

58. (C) Clouds shroud the planet Venus. These clouds trap the re-radiated long-wave energy. This is known as the "greenhouse effect".

59. (E) If all the planets resulted from a common origin, it is likely that they would all rotate in the same direction.

60. (A) Density is dependent upon the amount of matter and the space it occupies. Given Venus is the same size as earth, then the gravitational attraction is about equal on the surface which means something close to size of our atmosphere.

However, our atmosphere weighs 14 to 16 amu per atom (nitrogen = 14 and oxygen = 16). On Venus, the CO_2 = 44, H_2O = 18, and H_2SO_4 = 98 amu. So the composition of the atmosphere changes the total mass which means Venus' gravity pulls it closer to the surface of the planet thus increasing the density. The more dense, the greater the pressure because more collision between molecules takes place.